# VERVEINE

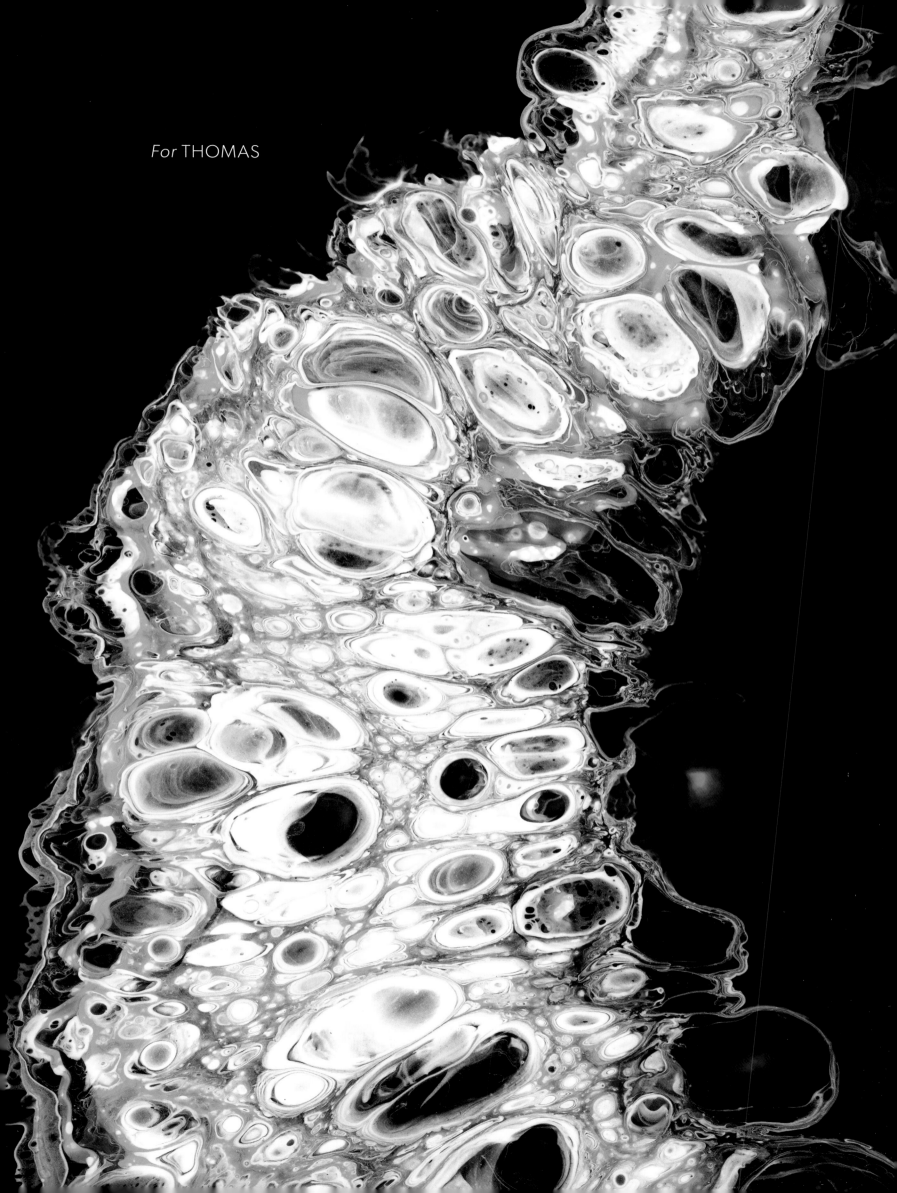

*For* THOMAS

# V E R V E I N E

## D A V I D   W Y K E S

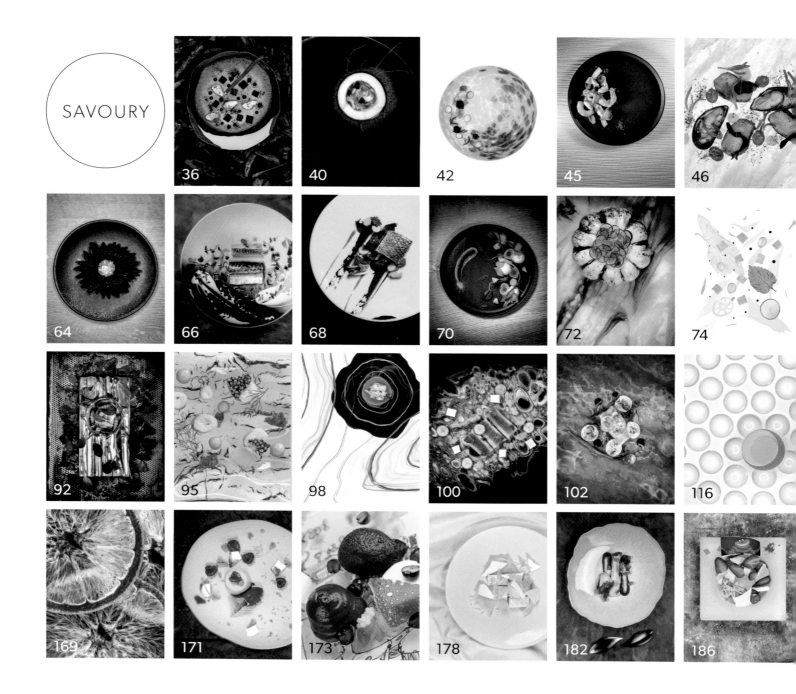

SAVOURY

36  40  42  45  46
64  66  68  70  72  74
92  95  98  100  102  116
169  171  173  178  182  186

RMC MEDIA

First published in Great Britain in 2018 by
RMC Media, 6 Broadfield Court, Sheffield, S8 0XF
Tel: 0114 250 6300
www.rmcmedia.co.uk

A CIP catalogue record for this book is
available from the British Library.

ISBN: 978-1-907998-34-8

Edited by Paul Orton and Martin Edwards

Photography by David Nash
www.theelectriceye.co.uk

Design by Steve Levers

Printed and bound by Gutenberg Press, Malta

# CONTENTS

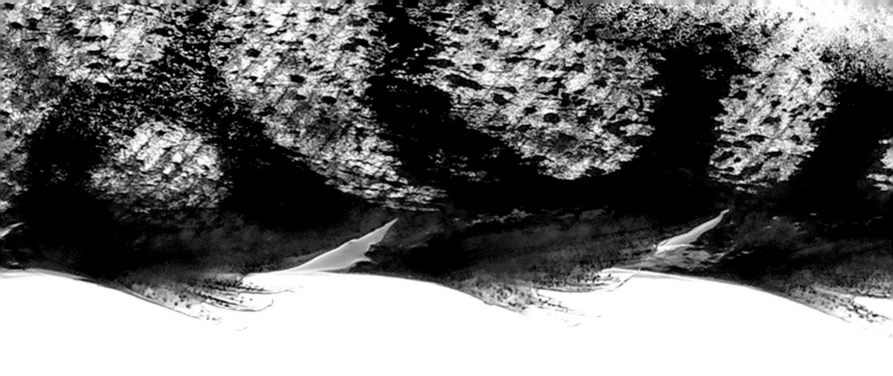

"*I don't do drugs, I am drugs*" S A L V A D O R   D A L I

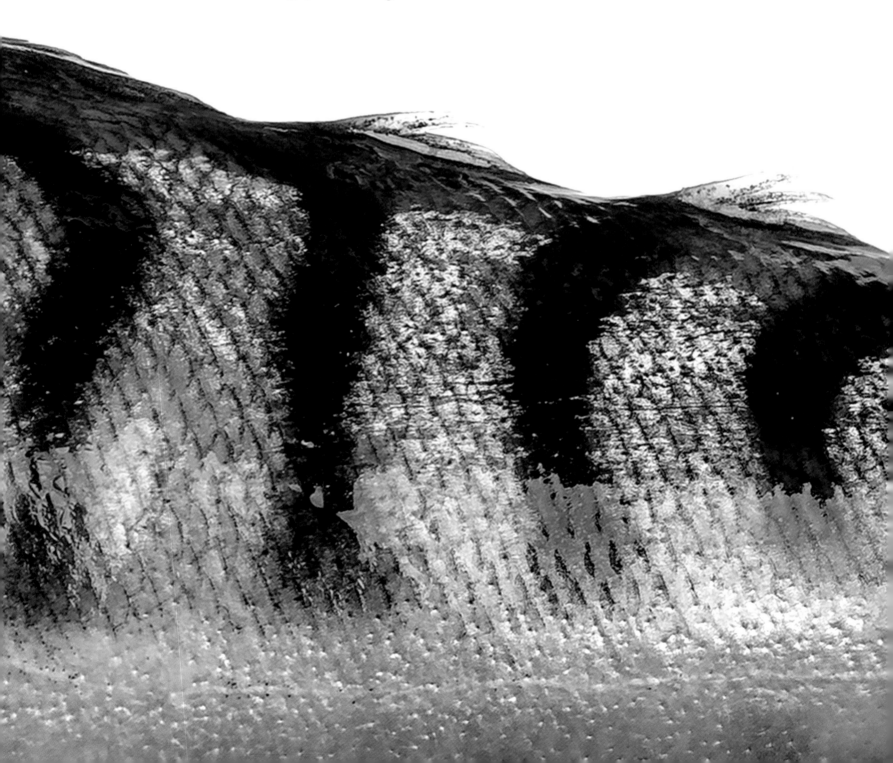

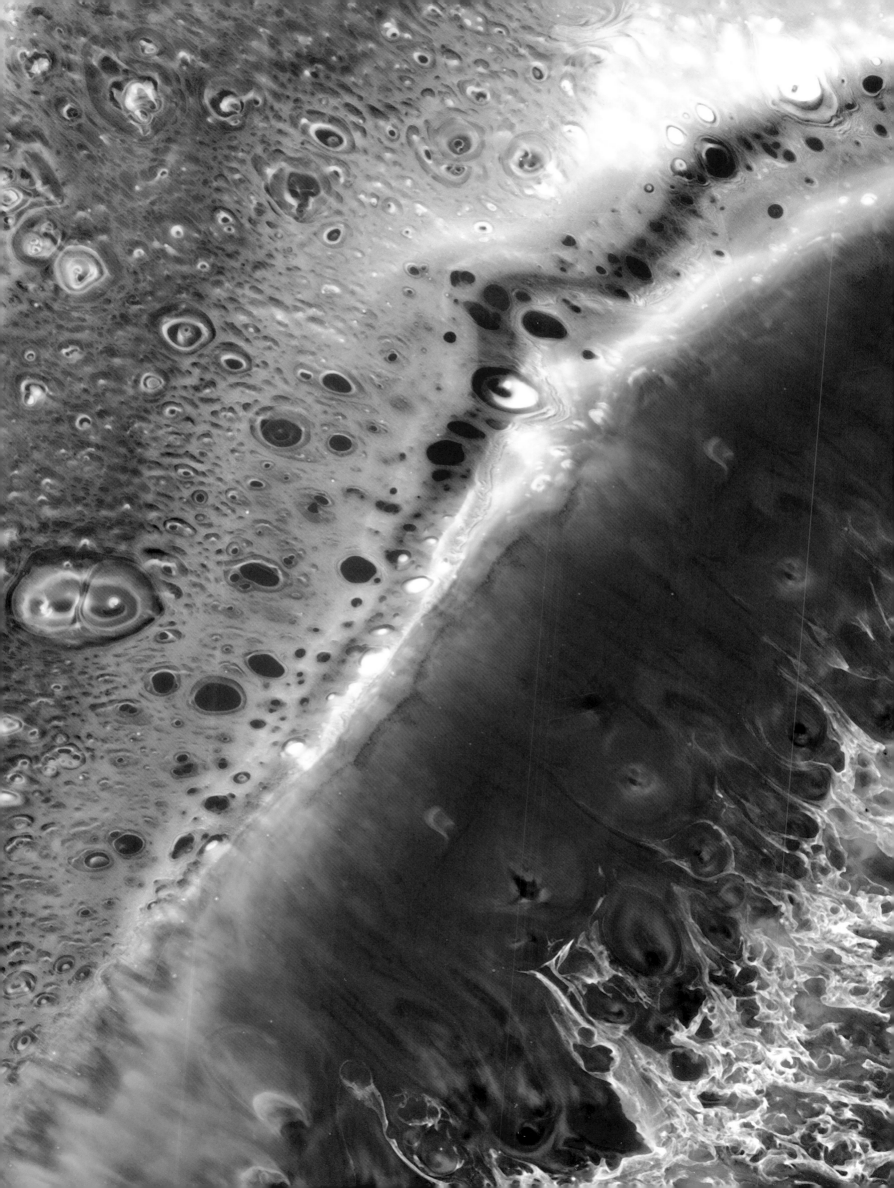

"*I'm playing all the right notes, but not necessarily in the right order*"

ERIC MORECAMBE

INTRODUCTION

Lemon Curd

1 lb lump sugar
½ lb fresh butter.
3. lemons.
6 eggs.

Method.

Melt sugar & butter in double saucepan
in basin in hot water. When sugar is warm
add well beaten eggs, leaving out 2 of the whites.
Stir in grated rind of 3 lemons and the juice
of 2, then stir all the time until it thickens
DO NOT BOIL.

Drink . Ginger Pear Shake.
Press a small tin of pears through a sieve and
add the juice to a quart of milk, Half fill six
tumblers with this mixture, and top with ginger ale

Table of Times for roa

| | | should be |
|---|---|---|
| Beef | 20 mins to the lb | + 20 m |
| Mutton " " " " | | |
| Pork | 30 mins " " " | |
| Veal | 25 mins " " " | + 30 mins |
| Rabbit | 15 mins " " " | + 25 mins |
| Chicken | 15 mins " " " | + 15 mins |
| lamb | 25 mins " " " | + 15 mins |
| | | + 25 mins |

This book is about expanding horizons.

It's a fundamental tool to provide the scope to think differently about food and to try combinations you might never have thought of.

The inspiration for it comes from 25 years in the kitchen, not to mention many late nights spent jotting in that which all chefs rely on – their notebook.

It's here that I have recorded every idea, every passing thought, every accidental discovery. My notebook is my blueprint for a new idea. It starts with random elements, fragments in themselves . But when assembled, they play a part in creating something. I always think it's rather like putting together the pieces of a mosaic. In the spirit of adventure, I stress this is only a guide, not a rulebook. So it would be false to say the recipes are as far as the creative process goes.

Experiment. Enjoy a new way of thinking about food.

David Wykes,
Verveine Restaurant, Hampshire
2018

# NOTES ON USING THIS BOOK

Cooking times are for guidance only, follow the manufacturer's instructions concerning temperatures if using a fan oven.

All eggs are medium in size.

All salt is fine sea salt (unless stated otherwise).

When no quantity is specified please use common sense.

All flour is plain unless stated otherwise.

All olive oil is Spanish extra virgin olive oil unless stated otherwise.

Any dishes that contain lightly cooked eggs should be avoided by anyone elderly, pregnant, infant, convalescents or with an impaired immune system.

When deep frying never leave the pan unattended, wear long sleeves and avoid any splashing when carefully adding food.

Some recipes in this book require some specialist ingredients or equipment, while it is possible to substitute these the end results may not be the same.

Exercise caution in any recipes using high temperatures, open flames or blow torches.

Mushrooms should be wiped clean.

All salads, herbs, seaweeds and vegetables should be washed before use.

Some recipes have been scaled down as far as possible for them to work correctly but may give you a larger quantity than needed.

All spoon measurements are level.

1 teaspoon = 5g
1 dessert spoon = 7.5g
1 tablespoon = 15g.

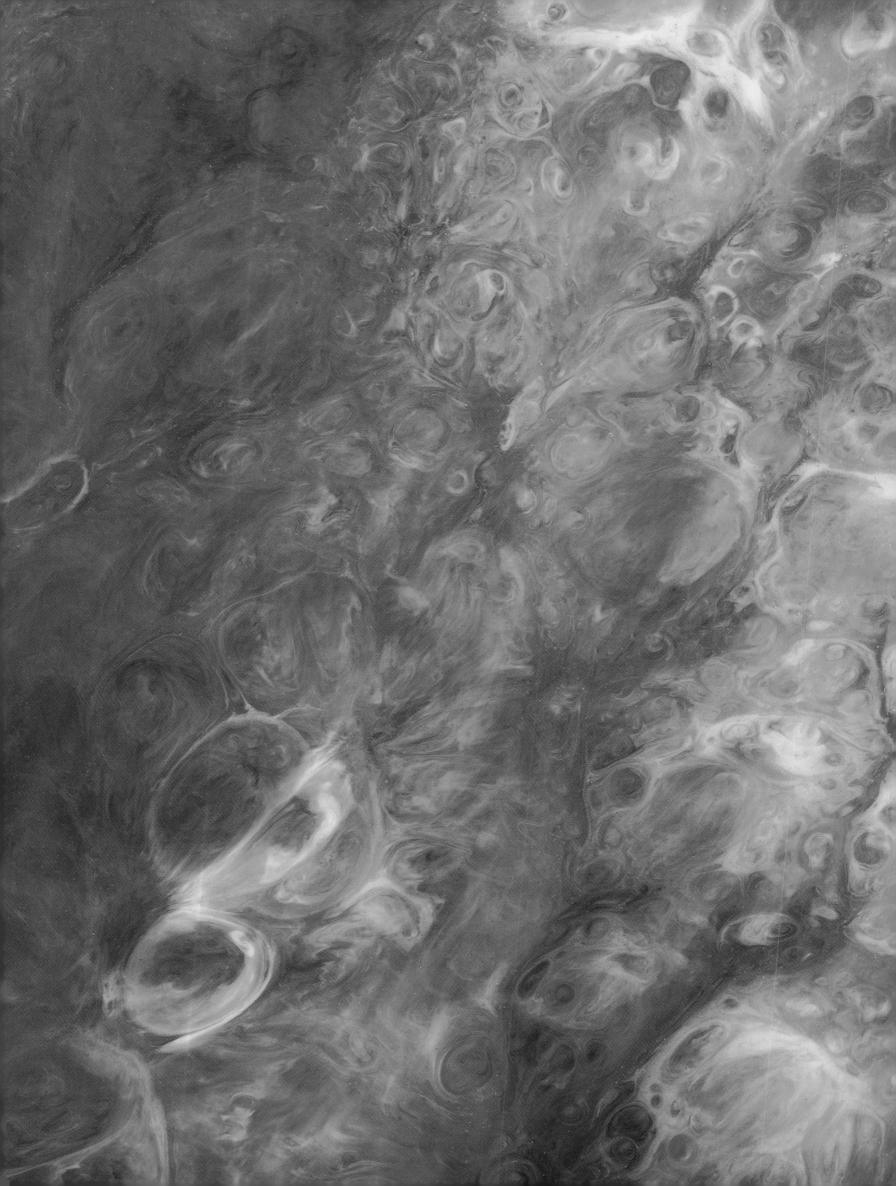

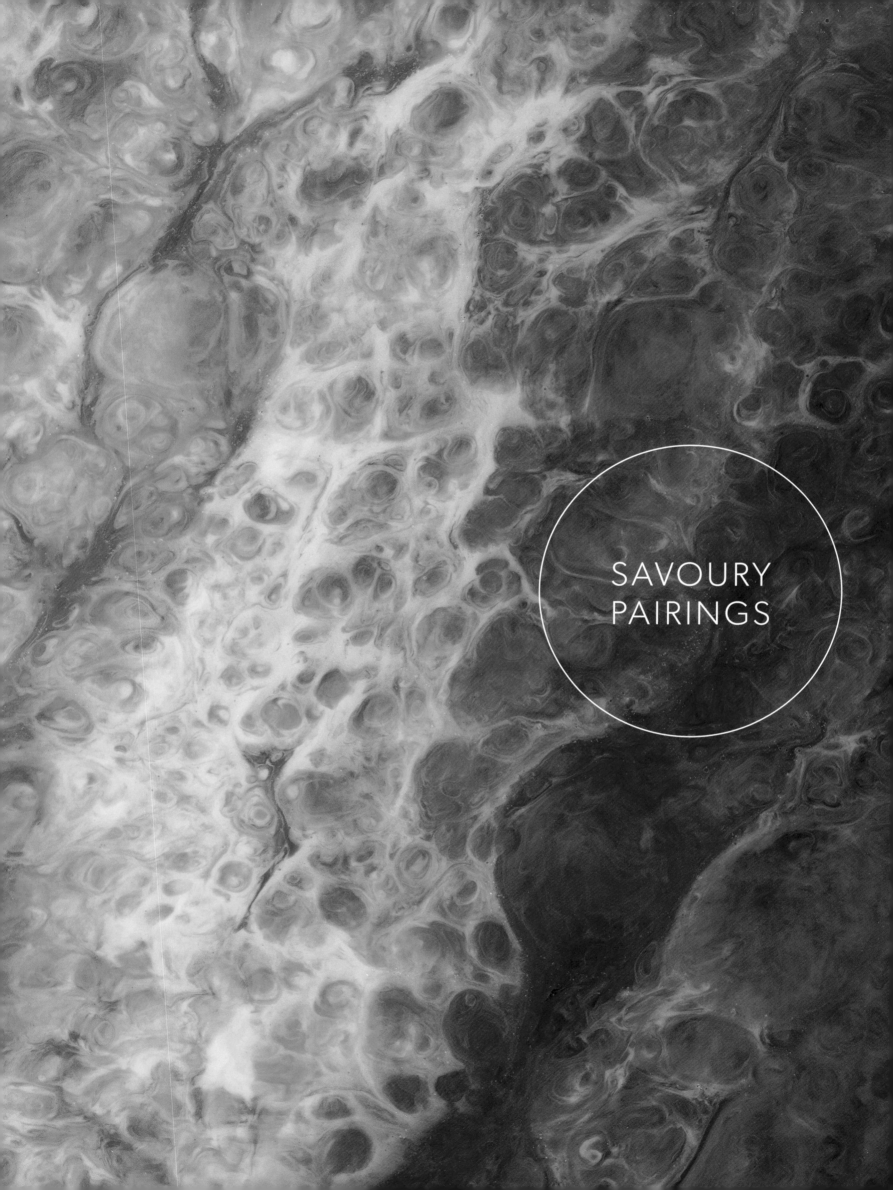

SAVOURY
PAIRINGS

## BRILL HALIBUT JOHN DORY SEA BASS TURBOT

Asparagus
Bacon
Butter
Capers
Citrus
Coconut
Cucumber
Dill
Fennel
Grape
Hard Cheese (especially Parmesan)
Hazelnut
Horseradish
Lardo
Mediterranean Vegetables
Morteau Sausage
Mushroom
Mustard
Olive Oil
Pale Lager
Parsley
Pasta
Pea
Potato
Prosciutto
Root Vegetables
Rosemary
Saffron
Shellfish
Shrimps (especially Brown)
Smoked Butter
Soy
Tarragon
Thyme
Verveine

## MACKEREL SALMON TUNA WILD SEA TROUT

Almond
Avocado
Beetroot
Chilli or Pepper
Citrus
Cucumber
Dill
Egg
Garlic, Black Garlic or Wild Garlic
Ginger
Gooseberry
Grapefruit
Hazelnut
Horseradish
Japanese Artichokes
Juniper
Leeks
Morteau Sausage
Mushroom
Olive Oil
Pea
Pineapple
Pork (especially Suckling Pig)
Radish
Rhubarb
Sesame
Sorrel
Soy
Thyme
Watercress

# COD
# HADDOCK
# MONKFISH

Artichokes
Asparagus
Bacon, Cured Pork
or Smoked Pork
Cabbage
Capers
Carrots
Chervil
Chorizo
Cider
Coriander
Cream
Fennel

Garlic
Shallots or Onion
Ginger
Leeks
Lemon
Lime
Merguez Sausage
Morteau Sausage
Mushrooms
Olives
Olive Oil
Parsley
Pasta
Peppers
Rosemary
Saffron

Soy
Thyme
Tomatoes
Vadouvan
(Mild Curry Spices)

# SMOKED FISH

Apple
Bacon
Caper
Coffee
Cabbage
(especially Pickled)
Coconut
Cherry
(especially Pickled)
Caviar
Citrus

Dill
Egg
Mild Curry Spice
Pea
Potato
Pasta
Soft Cheese
Watercress

# MUSSELS

Apricot
Anchovies
Bay
Breadcrumbs
Butter
Cayenne
Chervil
Chives
Chorizo
Curry
Fennel
Horseradish

Lamb
Leeks
Merguez Sausage
Orange
Parsnip
Pernod / Anise
Rice
Saffron
Seaweed
Vanilla
Watercress

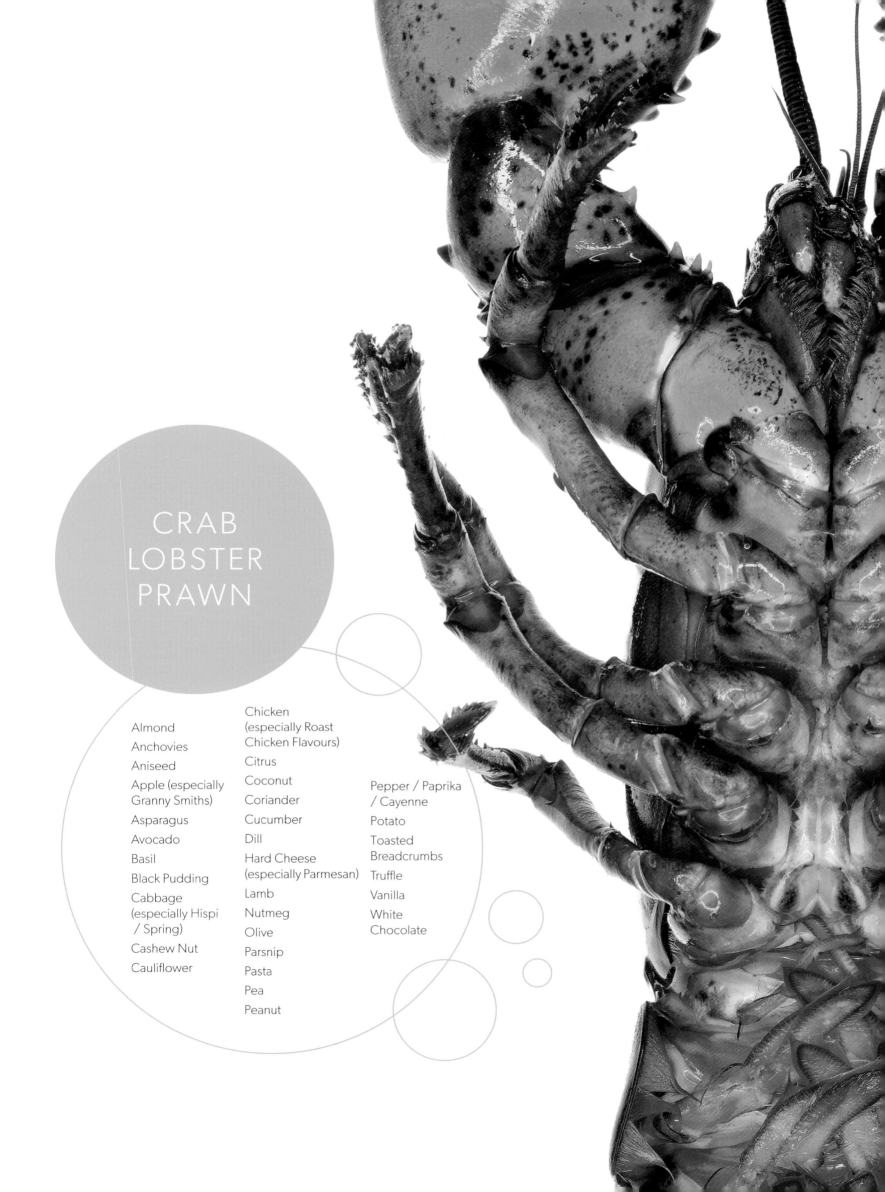

# CRAB
# LOBSTER
# PRAWN

Almond

Anchovies

Aniseed

Apple (especially
Granny Smiths)

Asparagus

Avocado

Basil

Black Pudding

Cabbage
(especially Hispi
/ Spring)

Cashew Nut

Cauliflower

Chicken
(especially Roast
Chicken Flavours)

Citrus

Coconut

Coriander

Cucumber

Dill

Hard Cheese
(especially Parmesan)

Lamb

Nutmeg

Olive

Parsnip

Pasta

Pea

Peanut

Pepper / Paprika
/ Cayenne

Potato

Toasted
Breadcrumbs

Truffle

Vanilla

White
Chocolate

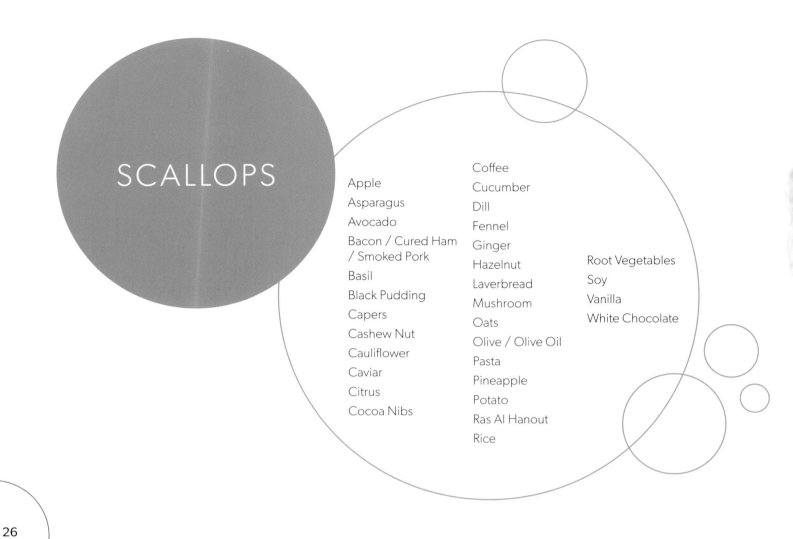

# SCALLOPS

Apple
Asparagus
Avocado
Bacon / Cured Ham / Smoked Pork
Basil
Black Pudding
Capers
Cashew Nut
Cauliflower
Caviar
Citrus
Cocoa Nibs
Coffee
Cucumber
Dill
Fennel
Ginger
Hazelnut
Laverbread
Mushroom
Oats
Olive / Olive Oil
Pasta
Pineapple
Potato
Ras Al Hanout
Rice
Root Vegetables
Soy
Vanilla
White Chocolate

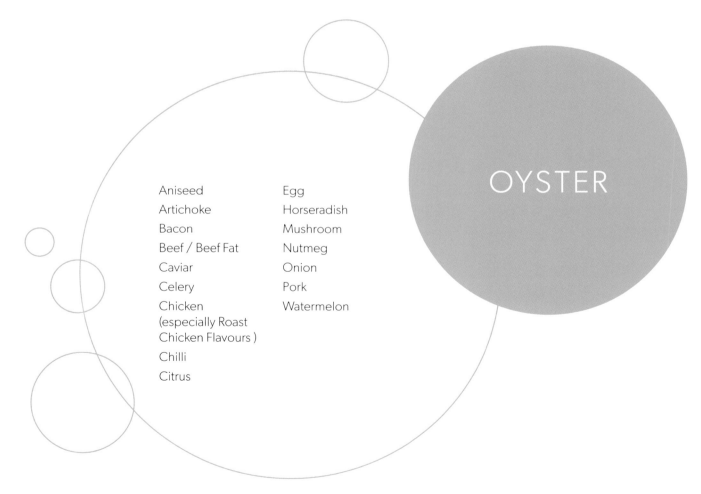

# OYSTER

Aniseed
Artichoke
Bacon
Beef / Beef Fat
Caviar
Celery
Chicken (especially Roast Chicken Flavours )
Chilli
Citrus
Egg
Horseradish
Mushroom
Nutmeg
Onion
Pork
Watermelon

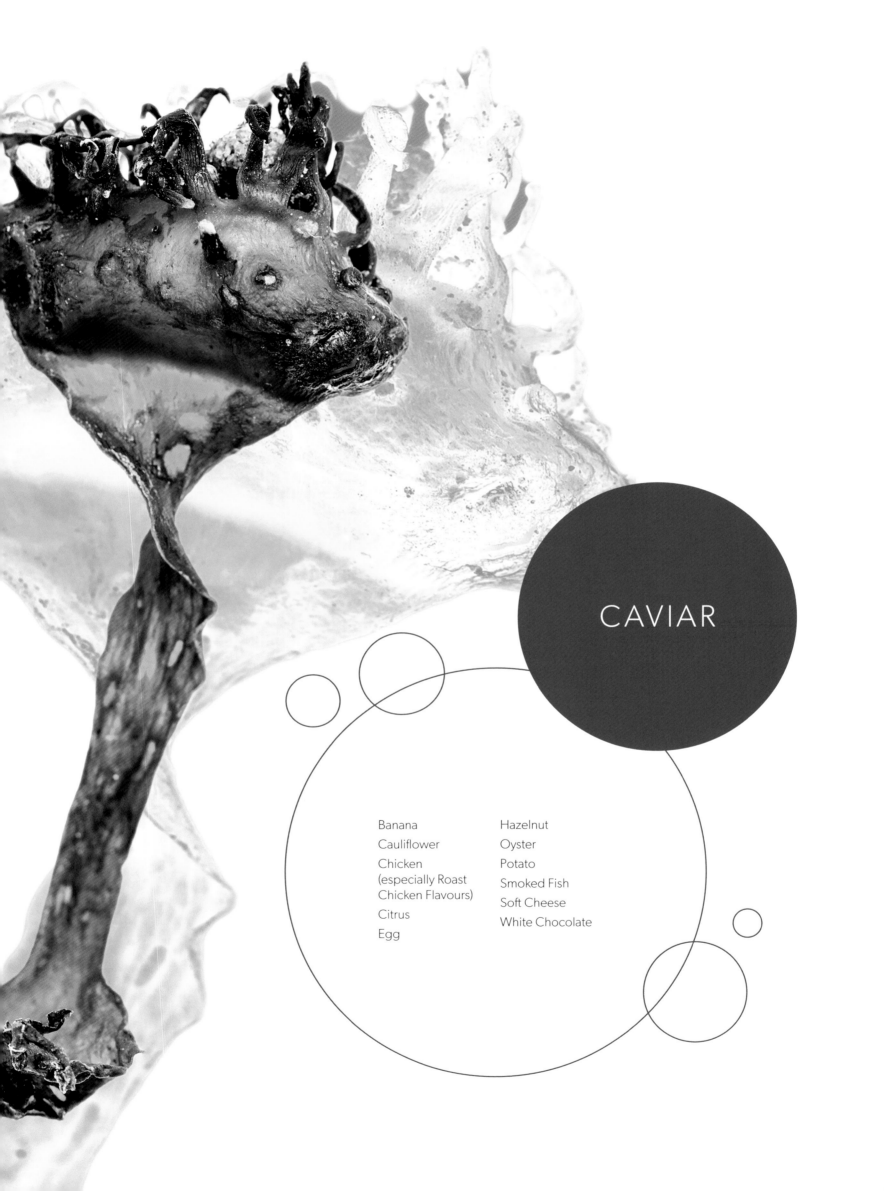

# CAVIAR

Banana
Cauliflower
Chicken
(especially Roast
Chicken Flavours)
Citrus
Egg

Hazelnut
Oyster
Potato
Smoked Fish
Soft Cheese
White Chocolate

# OCTOPUS
# SQUID

Basil
Bay
Beaujolais
Breadcrumbs
Campari
Citrus
Coriander
Fennel
Garlic
(especially Black)
Ginger
Merguez Sausage

Mint
Olive Oil
Onion
Parsley
Redcurrant
(especially Pickled)
Rosemary
Soy
Squid Ink
Tomato
White Wine

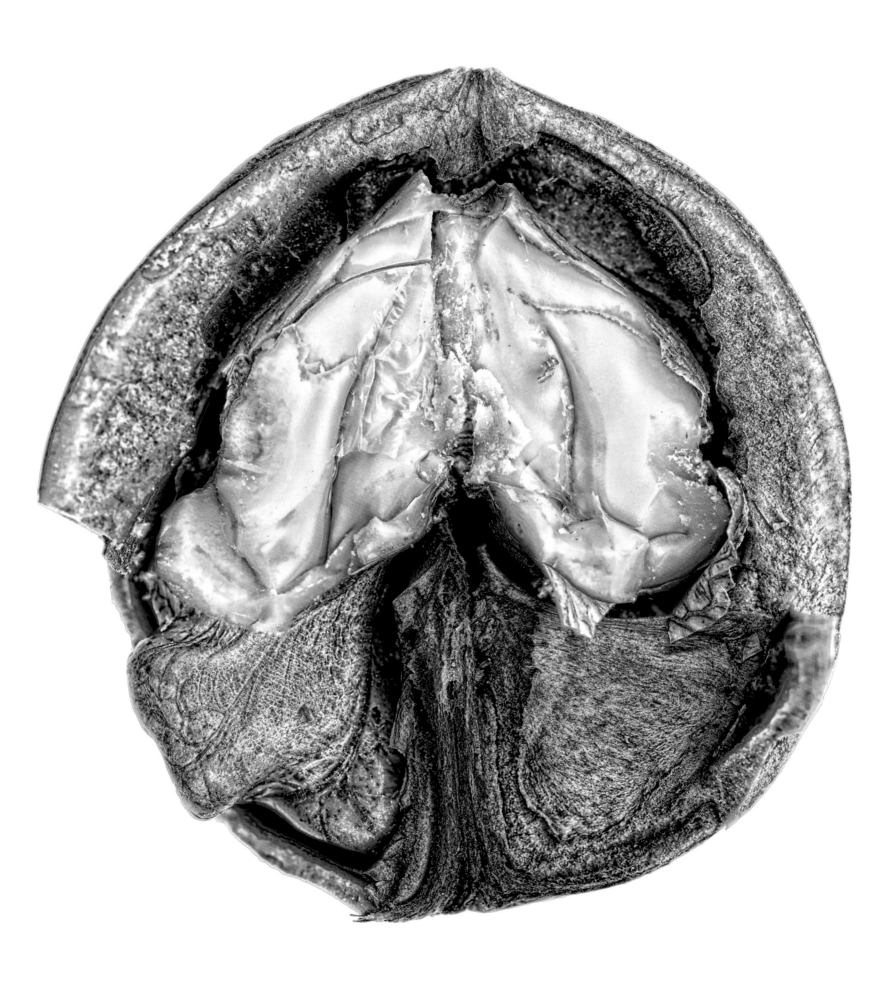

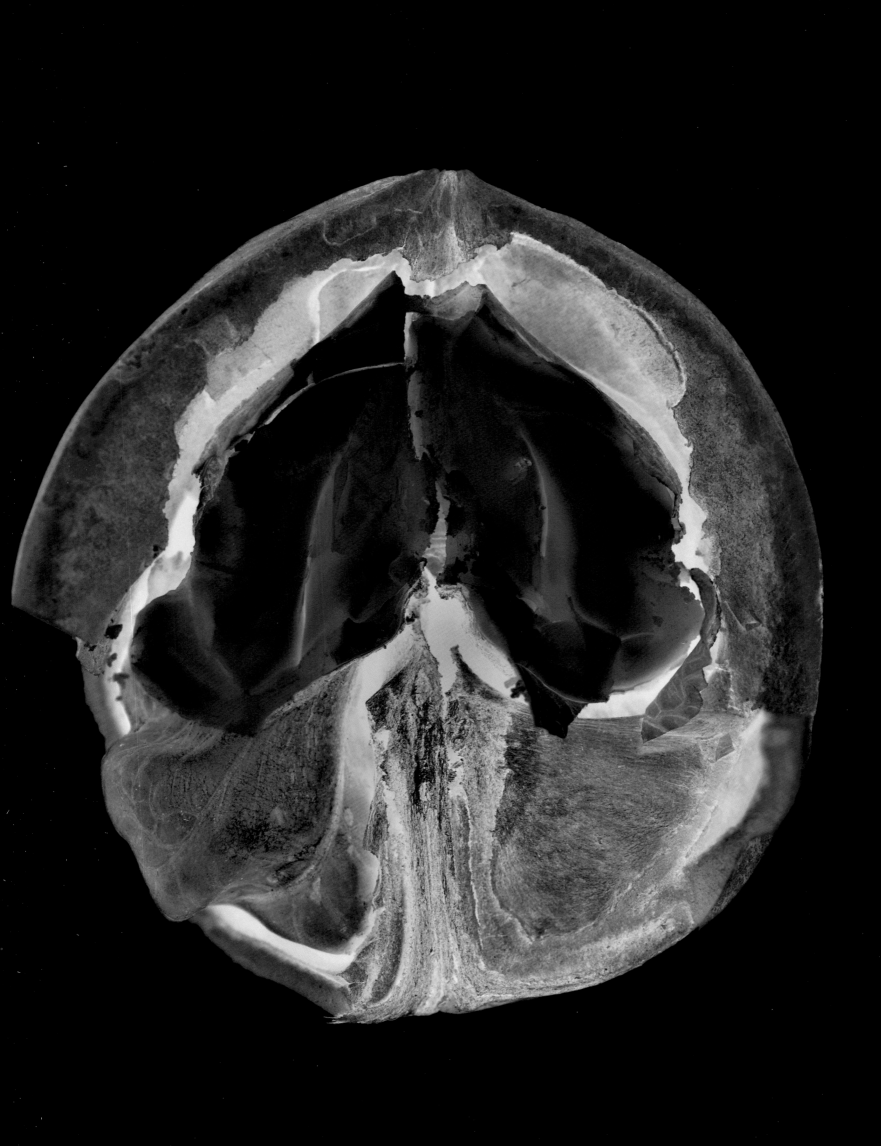

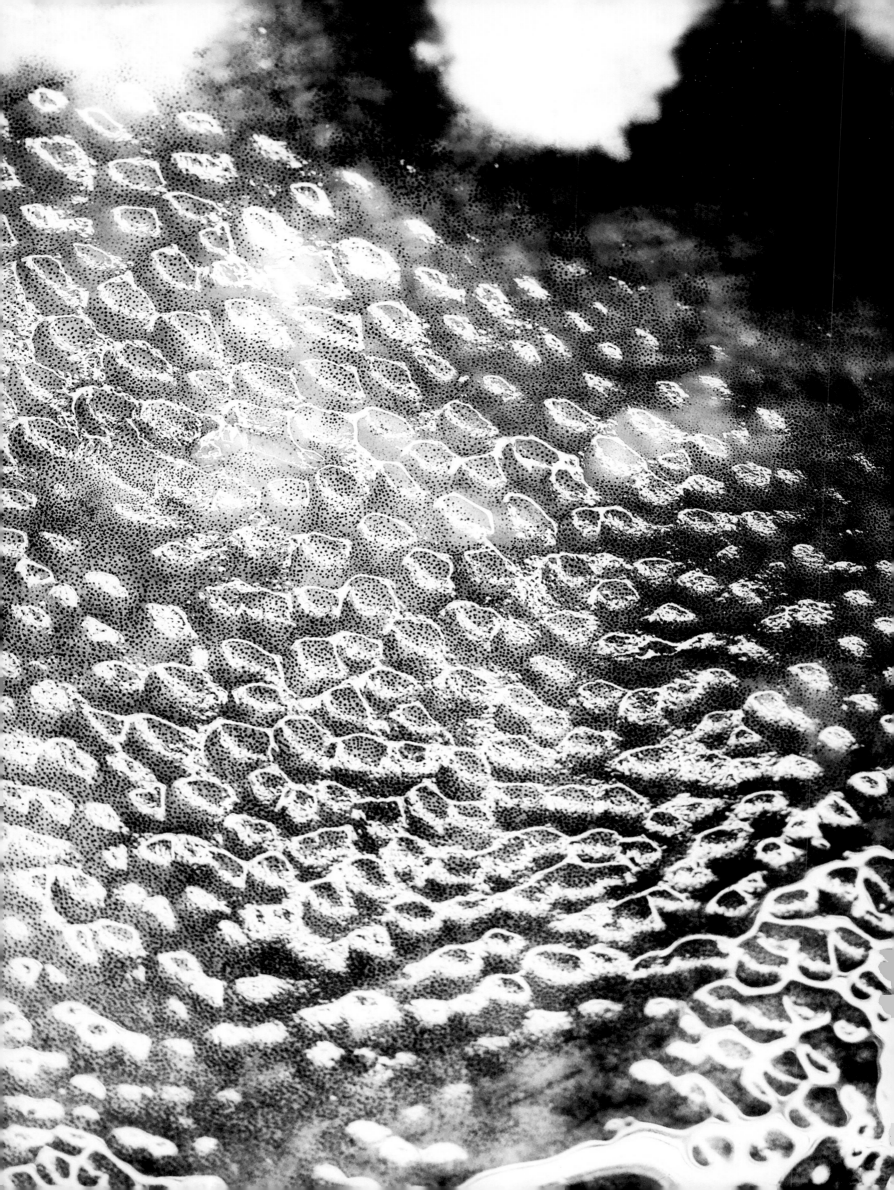

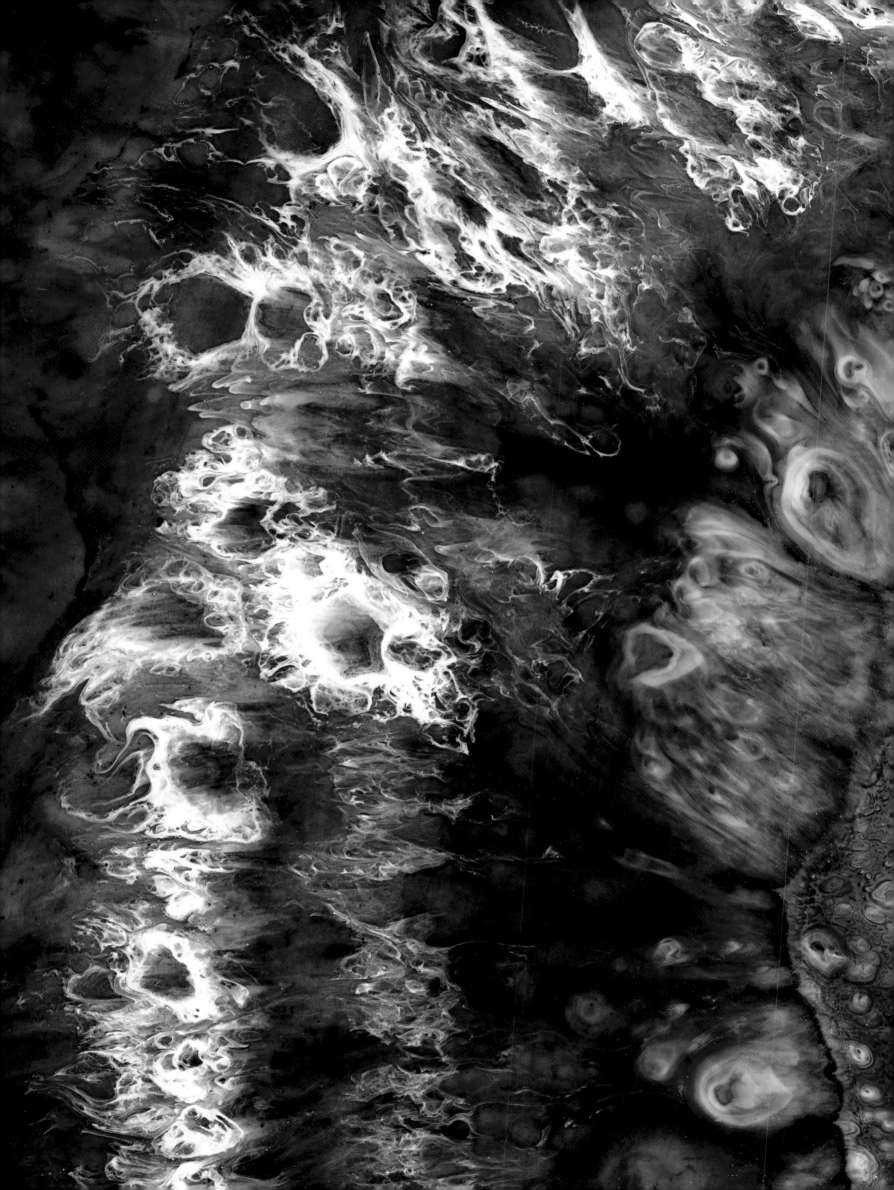

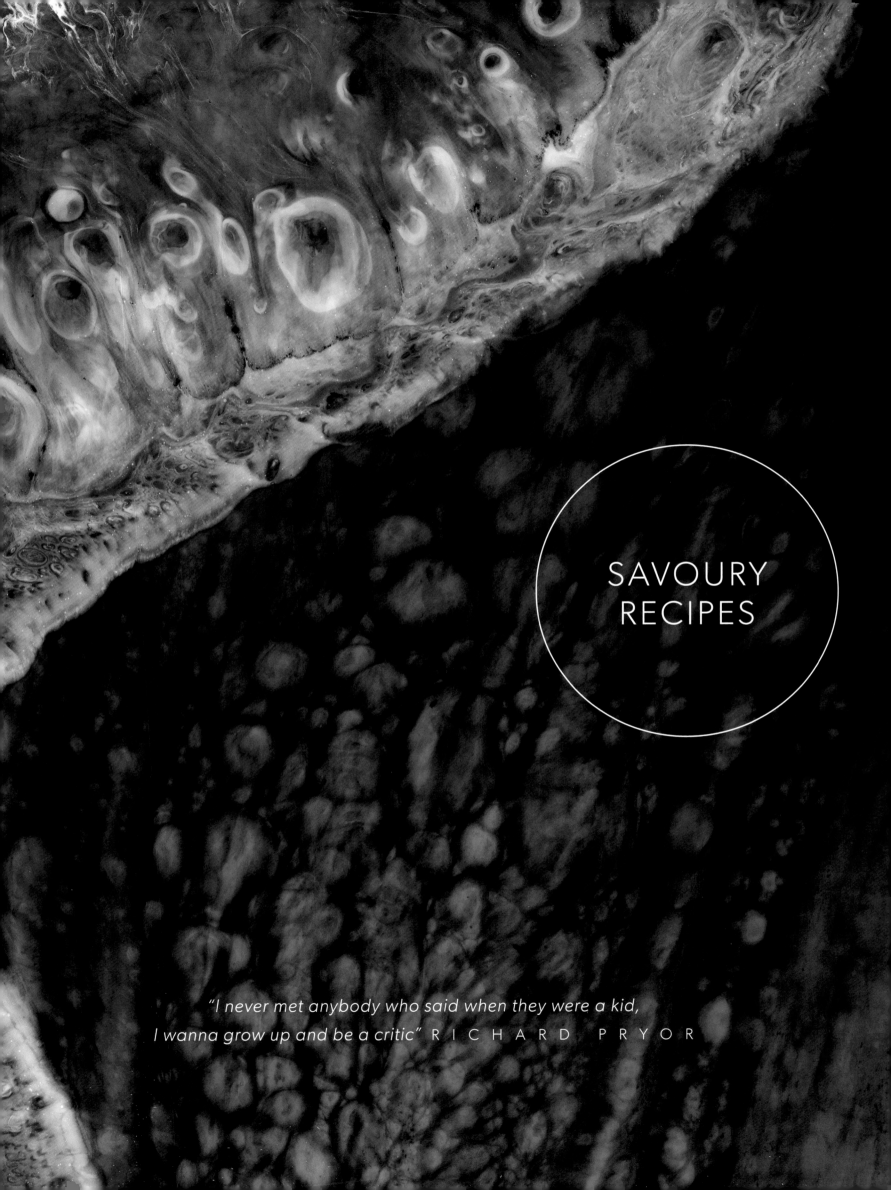

SAVOURY
RECIPES

*"I never met anybody who said when they were a kid,
I wanna grow up and be a critic"* RICHARD PRYOR

# SCALLOP, BONFIRE SOUNDS
# AND LIQUORICE SPEAR

## SCALLOPS

Scallops, 4 per person

Season the scallops with the coal salt and drizzle with the coal oil.
Cook on a plancha (or grill) until coloured, turn over and repeat.
Remove from the heat and finish with a little fresh lemon juice.

## BLACK PUDDING PURÉE

400g black pudding, in 1cm dice
50g unsalted butter
1 teaspoon fresh thyme, chopped
2 shallots, finely chopped
50g hazelnut oil
150g vegetable stock
Half a teaspoon xanthan gum (optional)
Seasoning

Melt the butter in a saucepan and add the shallots, sweat on a low heat for 2 minutes.
Add half the black pudding and thyme, fry for 1 minute.
Add the stock and bring to a simmer for 1 minute.
Season and transfer to a food processor, blend with the hazelnut oil.
Add the xanthan as required, check the seasoning and pass through a sieve.
Just before serving cook the diced pudding in a little unsalted butter, season and drain onto a lined tray.

## PICKLED GRANNY SMITH

2 Granny Smith apples
200g white vinegar
170g caster sugar
3 sprigs of thyme
Juice of 1 lemon

Peel and cut the apples into quarters.
Bring the vinegar, sugar and thyme to the boil.
Remove from the heat and chill.
When cold, add the apples and leave refrigerated for at least 6 hours before use.
Cut into 1cm dice.
Dry the diced apple on a J-cloth lined tray and roll in the ash.

## BURNT APPLE PURÉE

6 Granny Smiths
Water (as needed)
A few grains of sea salt
Half a teaspoon of xanthan gum

Preheat the oven to 190°C.
Roast the apples, every 30 minutes remove the tray from the oven and mush the apples together scraping from the sides, roast until a very dark caramel colour.
Remove from the oven and transfer to a blender.
Blend until smooth, adding enough water to loosen the cooked apples.
Season with a very small amount of salt, thicken with the xanthan gum and pass through a fine sieve.
Store in the refrigerator until needed.

*continued…*

*Scallop, Bonfire Sounds and Liquorice Spear continued...*

## ASH

1 bunch of dill
The green skin of one cucumber
The outer leaves of 2 leeks

Preheat the oven to 160°C.
On a dry heat (such as a barbecue or griddle pan), char all of the ingredients until black.
Place on a tray and dry in the oven until crispy.
Remove from the oven and leave to cool.
Blend in a food processor, pass through a sieve.
Store at room temperature in an airtight box.

## COAL SALT

250g Maldon sea salt
1 small lump of charcoal, about 20g
Zest of 1 lemon

Microplane the charcoal.
Mix all the ingredients together and keep in a sealed jar.

## COAL OIL

500ml olive oil
6 pieces charcoal

Get the charcoal burning by placing it over a gas hob.
Once it is lit, let it burn until it turns white and the flames go out.
Being careful not to burn yourself, take a pair of tongs and place the hot coals into the olive oil.
Leave to cool down, allowing the charcoal sediment to settle on the bottom of the pan.
Leave for at least 3 hours then gently pass the oil through a muslin cloth and store at room temperature until needed.

## TO SERVE

Liquorice sticks, sharpened to a point, 1 per person
Portable Bluetooth speaker
MP3 Player

Serve with the sharpened liquorice stick as cutlery.
Place a small portable Bluetooth speaker in a glass and cover with small pieces of burnt wood and coal and place on the serving table.
With a compatible device play the sound of a bonfire through the speaker (these MP3 files are readily available on online stores under Nature/Natural sounds).

# SCALLOPS, CONFIT RABBIT AND CARROT CAKE SAUCE

### SCALLOPS

4 scallops per person
Small nob of butter
Fresh lemon juice

Pan-fry the lightly seasoned scallops in a hot pan until golden on one side, gently turn over and continue to cook for another minute.

Remove from the heat, add the butter and lemon juice and baste for 30 seconds.

### CONFIT RABBIT

4 rabbit legs
Fine sea salt
Large bunch of thyme
500g duck fat

The day before using, place the rabbit legs in a non-reactive container (plastic or stainless steel).

Sprinkle the rabbit legs with salt and scatter half the thyme over the legs.

Leave covered in the fridge for 24 hours.

The next day thoroughly wash the rabbit legs with cold water, pat dry and lay in an ovenproof dish.

Preheat the oven to 120°C.

Cover with the duck fat and add the rest of the thyme.

Seal with a tight-fitting lid and cook in the oven for 5 hours (or until falling away from the bone).

Remove from the oven, cool slightly and remove from the fat (this fat can be used several times for confit).

Pick the meat, discarding any fat or sinew.

Check for seasoning and add a dessert spoon of the duck fat into the meat.

Mix well and press into a cling film lined mould.

Place a heavy object onto the rabbit to press.

Chill until set.

### CARROT CAKE SAUCE

35g caster sugar
90g white flour
1½ teaspoons baking powder
1½ teaspoons cinnamon
Salt
75g oil
235g grated carrot
3 whole eggs

Blend all the ingredients in a food processor until smooth.

Empty the purée into a small pan and on a low heat bring the temperature up to 80°C, stirring all the time.

Pass through a fine sieve and store in an airtight container.

### TO SERVE

5 slices of pickled carrots per person
Micro lemon balm cress to garnish

# CRAB, COCONUT, PARSNIP
# AND CASHEW

### CRAB

1 brown cock crab, about 1kg
(those from the west country are best)
A little lemon juice

*Shell fish is best cooked in heavily salted water, this makes the water more dense which won't penetrate the shell.*

Plunge the crab into heavily salted boiling water, cook for 9 minutes.
Refresh in cold water and drain.
Crack the claws and the top joint of the smaller legs, reserving the meat in the body for another recipe.
Pick through the white meat, checking for pieces of shell.
Season with a little lemon juice, salt and a few drops of olive oil.
Keep chilled until needed.

### COCONUT

1 medium sized coconut

Crack the coconut and remove the husk.
Peel the coconut flesh thinly and lightly toast in a dry frying pan.

### PARSNIP CRISPS

1 parsnip, peeled into strips using a wide blade speed peeler
Deep-fat fryer preheated to 180°C

Deep-fry the parsnip strips in a deep-fat fryer until a light golden brown.
Remove from the oil and drain any excess oil on a paper towel lined tray.
Season with a little fine sea salt.

### CASHEWS

150g unsalted cashew nuts
Worcestershire sauce salt
Olive oil

Toss the cashews in a frying pan over a medium heat with a little olive oil.
Season with the Worcestershire sauce salt.
Drain any excess oil onto a paper towel lined tray.

### WORCESTERSHIRE SAUCE SALT

350g sea salt
65g Worcestershire sauce

Mix the two ingredients together.
Place on a lined tray and dehydrate on 45°C until dry (about 6 hours).
Blend until fine.

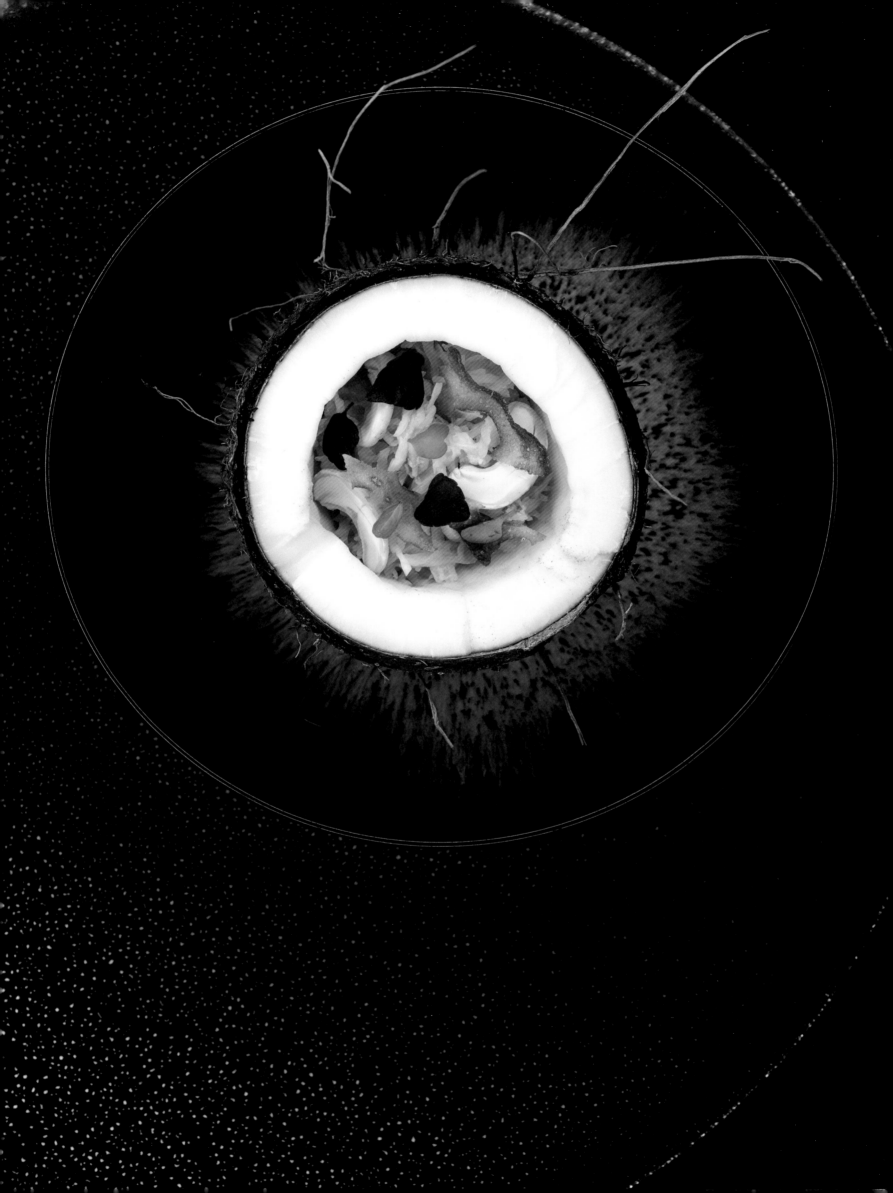

# CRAB, COMPRESSED WATERMELON, RADISH AND YUZU

## CRAB

1 brown cock crab, about 1kg
(those from the west country are best)
A little lemon juice

Plunge the crab into heavily salted boiling water, cook for 9 minutes.

Refresh in cold water and drain.

Crack the claws and the top joint of the smaller legs, reserving the meat in the body for another recipe.

Pick through the white meat, checking for pieces of shell.

Season with a little lemon juice, salt and a few drops of olive oil.

Keep chilled until needed.

## YUZU DRESSING

200g extra virgin olive oil
50g yuzu juice
Fine sea salt

Mix all the ingredients together and store in the fridge in a plastic bottle until needed.

Shake well before use.

## RADISH

3 breakfast radishes, leaves removed

Slice the radishes very thinly and store in iced water until needed.

## COMPRESSED WATERMELON

5 slices of watermelon, 2cm thick, seeds removed

Freeze the watermelon on a tray for 24 hours.

Defrost with a reasonably heavy object on top (this will push out any excess moisture).

Pat dry with a J-cloth, transfer to a dehydrator and dry for 12 hours (this can be done well in advance and stored in the fridge in an airtight box for up to a week).

## PICKLED WATERMELON

2 slices of watermelon, 1cm thick
100g Minus 8 maple verjus
20g cider vinegar
A few grams of sea salt

Place all the ingredients in a vac pac bag and seal on 100% vacuum, repeat this twice.

After the final time, leave refrigerated for at least 4 hours before use.

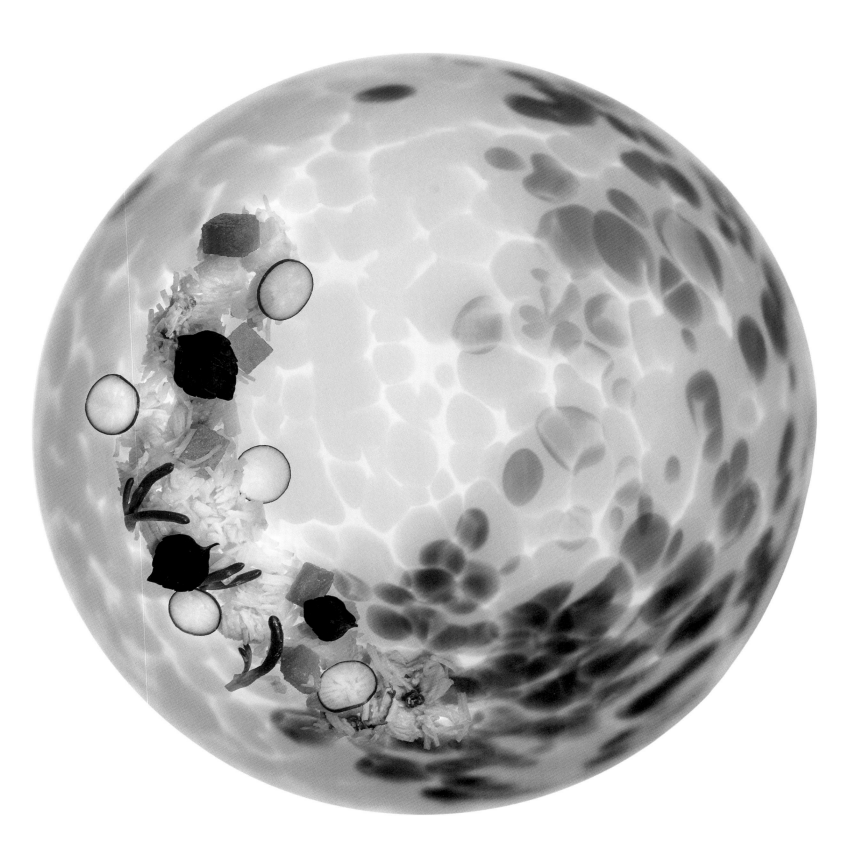

# GALICIAN PRAWNS, PORK SKIN, SATAY AND COCONUT

## PRAWNS

16 Galician prawns, heads removed but not peeled (heads kept to one side)
Fine sea salt

Seal the prawn tails in a vac pac bag with a good pinch of fine sea salt. Cook in a water bath set at 62°C for 30 minutes.
Refresh the bags in iced water.
Peel the prawns, keeping the shells.
Run a knife around the back of the tail and devein.
Keep in the fridge in an airtight box until needed.

## PORK SKIN

1 skin from a pork loin with as much fat removed as possible

Place the pork skin in a pan, cover with lightly salted water and simmer for 2 hours.
Remove from the heat and cool slightly.
Remove the skin from the water (discard the water) and lay flat on a lined tray. Refrigerate overnight.
Next day transfer the pork to a chopping board and scrape off any remaining fat.
Cut the skin into 5cm squares.
Dehydrate for 20 hours on 60°C.
Pan dry (at this stage the pork skins can be kept at room temperature in a box with a tight-fitting lid for up to 2 weeks).
Heat a fryer to 180°C and fry the dried pork skins (they will treble in size).
Remove from the fat onto a lined tray to absorb any excess fat.
Season and garnish with small coriander micro shoots.

## SATAY

3 dessert spoons honey
3 dessert spoons coconut oil
6 shallots, chopped
1 dessert spoon satay seasoning
4 cloves of garlic, finely chopped
400g peanut butter
2 tins coconut milk
100g (approximately) light soy sauce
50g (approximately) fish sauce

Fry off the shallots and garlic in the coconut oil, add the other ingredients.
Gently simmer and blend in a food processor until smooth.
Check seasoning.

## EDIBLE SHELLS

Shells from the tails
300g water
200g caster sugar
2 large sprigs of rosemary
2 large sprigs of thyme

In a small saucepan boil the water and sugar.
Remove from the heat and chill.
Add the herbs.
Vac pac the shells and the herb syrup on 100% and refrigerate for 2 days.
Drain and pat dry.
Cook on a lined tray in a preheated oven at 160°C until golden (about 12 minutes).

## PRAWN POWDER

Prawn heads
Extra virgin olive oil
Rosemary
Thyme
Lemon zest
Fine sea salt

Preheated oven on 200°C.
In a frying pan sauté the prawn heads, season and add the herbs and the zest.
Roast in the oven for 15 minutes.
Transfer to a tray and dehydrate for 12 hours at 60°C.
Blend in a spice grinder and pass through a fine sieve.
Keep in an airtight container until needed.

## COCONUT

1 medium coconut

Crack the coconut and remove the husk.
Peel the coconut flesh thinly and lightly toast in a dry frying pan.

# LAMB, MUSSELS, SOUR APRICOT AND BEACH HERBS

### LAMB

1 cannon of lamb, skin and fat removed
Seasoning
A small amount olive oil
1 sprig of rosemary

In a hot pan add the oil and seal the lamb.

Colour on both sides, turn the heat down and add the butter, baste with a spoon and cook until pink (in total about 8 minutes).

(Alternatively vac pac the seasoned lamb with a small amount of oil and the rosemary, place in water bath at 54°C for 13 minutes, remove from the bag, pat dry with a clean J-cloth and baste with foaming butter for 2 minutes on a medium to high heat).

### MUSSELS

400g mussels, cleaned and bearded
200g dry white wine
2 shallots, peeled and finely diced
A little butter
Extra virgin olive oil, to dress
Lemon juice, to dress

Melt the butter in a medium sized pan on a low heat, add the shallot and sweat for a minute without colour.

Add the wine, turn up the heat and bring to the boil.

Add the mussels, put the lid on and shake the pan.

Steam the mussels until they are open, discarding any that stay closed.

Refresh under cold water and pick from the shells.

Chill until needed.

Just before plating, dress with a little extra virgin olive oil, fresh lemon juice and sea salt.

### APRICOT

150g dried apricots
Enough water to cover
35g white wine vinegar

Place the apricots in a pan, cover with cold water and simmer until soft (about 35 minutes, you may need to top the water up).

Cool slightly and purée until smooth in a food processor with the white wine vinegar.

Pass through a sieve.

## EDIBLE MUSSEL SHELLS

200g pasta flour
100g water
20g squid ink
5g fine sea salt
40 mussel shell halves, emptied, cleaned and completely dried

Make a smooth black dough from the first four ingredients, cover with cling film and leave to rest in the fridge for at least 4 hours.

Oil the mussel shells liberally.

Roll the dough through a pasta machine.

Using two mussel shells that fit tightly together, press the dough onto the shells, making sure it overlaps the lips of the shells.

Fry at 180°C for a few minutes.

(The shells will need a little pressure to hold them together for the first minute or so of cooking; we use the tips of plating tweezers, but be extremely careful not to burn yourself).

## BEACH HERBS

Sea purslane
Sea kale
Samphire

# LANGOUSTINE, CELERIAC, PARMESAN AND MUSTARD AGNOLOTTI AND MUSHROOM POWDER

## LANGOUSTINES

**Langoustines (4 per person)**

Separate the head from the tails (the heads can be frozen and used for another recipe).

Peel the tails and remove the digestive tract.

Lightly wash in iced water and store in a J-cloth lined box in the fridge until needed.

## FOR THE AGNOLOTTI

## PASTA DOUGH

300g flour
15g fine sea salt
160g egg yolks
1 whole egg
1 tablespoon extra virgin olive oil

Mix the salt and the flour together.

Make a well in the centre of the flour and add the yolks, eggs and oil.

Work all the ingredients to a smooth dough and knead for ten minutes.

Rest for at least an hour.

Depending on the humidity of the flour, the pasta will sometimes need a little more egg yolk or flour; the dough should be soft and supple.

## FILLING

400g water
5g fine sea salt
30g salted butter
20g extra virgin olive oil
55g polenta
70g finely grated Parmesan
20g chopped rosemary and thyme
2 teaspoons grain mustard

Bring the water and salt to the boil.

Sprinkle in the polenta and the herbs and whisk.

Turn the heat down low and cook for 25 minutes.

Remove from the heat and cool slightly.

Transfer to a food blender and turn on medium.

Add all the other ingredients and blend until smooth.

Check seasoning, chill until set.

Transfer to a piping bag.

Using a pasta machine roll out the pasta twice on the thickest setting, then roll through the different settings twice on each one right to the thinnest.

Pipe a line of the filling 3cm in from the edge along the length of the sheet of pasta and roll the pasta over, encasing the filling.

Pinch the filling at 3cm gaps.

Using a pasta wheel cutter, cut the strip of agnolottis lengthways, then cut through the pinch marks.

Store on a little polenta in the fridge until needed.

Cook in simmering salted water for 1 minute (boiling water is a little too harsh for the delicate nature of filled fresh egg pasta).

## CELERIAC PURÉE

1 celeriac, peeled
2 shallots, peeled
350g double cream
Extra virgin olive
1 teaspoon xanthan gum (optional)

In a medium saucepan sauté the shallots in the olive oil.
Add the celeriac and brown, then add the cream.
Top up with water to cover and simmer until soft.
Transfer to blender and purée until smooth.
Add the xanthan gum, if using, and check the seasoning.
Pass through a fine sieve.
Keep warm until needed (the purée can be kept in the fridge for up to 3 days).

## MUSHROOM POWDER

*Mushroom powder will work with any mushrooms. At Verveine we use ceps, trompettes or morels.*

Place your sliced mushrooms on a lined dehydrator tray and dry at 40°C until crispy (about 8-10 hours).
Transfer to a coffee or spice grinder, add a pinch of sea salt and blend until smooth.
Pass through a fine sieve.
This powder will keep at room temperature in an airtight box for 1 month.
(Alternatively you can buy wild mushroom powder from fine food shops).

## TO SERVE

Drizzle a little extra virgin olive oil over the langoustine tails and season.
Cook for 1 minute each side on a plancha (or grill).
Finish with a little fresh lemon juice.

# LOBSTER, WHITE CHOCOLATE, PATA NEGRA AND PASSION FRUIT

1 x 750g lobster
Lemon juice
Extra virgin olive oil
Seasoning
Pea shoots
100g pata negra ham, sliced
50g piece of white chocolate
Seeds from 1 passion fruit

## LOBSTER

Cook the lobster in a large pan of boiling salted water for
9 minutes, refresh in iced water, drain and chill.

Remove the tail from the body, crack the tail shell and remove
the flesh.

Remove the claws and crack with back end of a knife, carefully
remove the claw meat.

Slice thinly and season with a little extra virgin olive oil, salt
and a few drops of fresh lemon juice.

## PEA SHOOTS

Dress the pea shoots in a few drops of olive oil.

## PICKLED CARROTS

200g caster sugar
200g white wine vinegar
2 medium sized carrots sliced thinly

Bring the white wine vinegar and caster sugar to the boil.
Remove from the heat and leave to cool for 1 minute.
Pour onto the carrots and leave to cool.
Store in an airtight box in the refrigerator until needed.

## TO SERVE

Place the lightly dressed lobster onto the plate, add the pata
negra and the pea shoots.

Drain a few slices of pickled carrot with a J-cloth.

Spoon a few seeds of passion fruit over the plate and finish
with a small amount of finely grated white chocolate.

# SLOW COOKED OCTOPUS, CHORIZO, PRESERVED LEMONS AND CRISPY CHICKEN SKIN

## OCTOPUS

1 mediterranean octopus
250g dry white wine
Seasoning

In a large pan cover the octopus with the wine and water, season well.

Bring up to the boil, turn down the heat and simmer until tender (about 4 or 5 hours).

When cooked, cool slightly in the water, then remove.

When cold enough to handle, remove the suckers and outside membrane.

Wash under cold water and refrigerate for 2 hours.

Slice thinly (this will keep in the fridge for 3 days).

## CHORIZO

1 small good quality chorizo, finely diced
A few sprigs of fresh thyme
250g extra virgin olive oil

In a pan, combine the ingredients and leave over a gentle heat for 7-8 minutes, remove and keep in an airtight box in the fridge.

## PRESERVED LEMONS

300g unwaxed untreated medium lemons
Fine sea salt
110g freshly squeezed lemon and lime juice
100g extra virgin olive oil

Wash the lemons well, remove any blemishes and cut into quarters lengthways, but don't cut all the way through.

Sprinkle fine sea salt into each cut surface and close.

Seal in a vac pac bag for 3 days and leave in an ambient temperature.

Open the bag and add the lemon and lime juice and the olive oil, seal the bag again and keep chilled for four weeks.

Cut and rinse well before using.

## CRISPY CHICKEN SKIN

Chicken skin from the breast
Seasoning

Preheat the oven to 150°C.

Remove all the excess lumps of fat from the underside of the skin by scraping with the side of a medium sized kitchen knife.

Lay the skin completely flat on a non-stick mat on a baking tray.

Lightly season the skin and place another non-stick mat and another baking tray on top (this will keep the skin flat and also squeeze the fat from the skin).

Place in the oven until golden brown (about 40 minutes).

Remove from the oven, remove the top tray and the top mat and leave to cool.

Store in an airtight box at room temperature for up to 3 days.

## DRESSING

2 teaspoons Minus 8 maple verjus vinegar
Fine sea salt
Extra virgin olive oil, to taste

In a bowl add the diced preserved lemons, chorizo and the octopus.

Lightly season and add a few drops of maple verjus vinegar to taste.

## TO SERVE

Slice the octopus finely and finish with a little olive oil and lemon juice.

Dice some of the preserved lemon and add.

Add the chorizo.

Lightly season and add a few drops of the dressing to taste.

Break pieces of the chicken skin over the top.

# PRAWN COCKTAIL AND
# BUTTERED TOAST ICE CREAM

## PRAWNS

500g peeled north Atlantic prawns

*(It is always best to peel these yourself as they have a much better flavour than ready-peeled prawns, and you are reserving the shells for the prawn and paprika powder)*

**Olive oil**

**Fresh lemon juice**

**Fine sea salt**

**2 baby gem lettuces, washed, leaves cut in half lengthways**

Just before serving, season the prawns with the lemon, extra virgin olive oil and sea salt.

## CANDIED CHERRY TOMATOES

Cherry tomatoes scored, blanched and peeled

Caster sugar

Roll the peeled cherry tomatoes in the caster sugar, place on lined tray and leave to dry in a dehydrator on 52°c until the tomatoes have half dried (about 8 hours).

These can be stored in extra virgin olive in the fridge for up to 2 months.

## CUCUMBER GRANITE

1 cucumber, seeds removed
(reserve the seeds for the charred seeds below)

Juice the cucumber in a food processor or juicer and season.

Freeze in a plastic container until solid.

Reserve in the freezer.

A couple of hours before serving scrape with a fork to obtain small, smooth ice crystals.

Serve frozen.

## MARIE ROSE ESPUMA

100g egg yolks

1 teaspoon french mustard

500g sunflower or rapeseed oil

Seasoning

1 dessert spoon white wine vinegar

1 dessert spoon water

30g tomato ketchup

12 drops Worcestershire sauce (you can add more or less of the tomato ketchup and Worcestershire sauce depending on taste)

500ml foam canister with 1 x $N_2O$ charge

In a food blender blitz the yolks, mustard and slowly add the oil, then all the other ingredients to taste.

Transfer to a foam gun and charge with the $N_2O$.

Keep chilled for at least 4 hours before use.

This sauce can be kept refrigerated in the canister for 3 days.

## PRAWN AND PAPRIKA POWDER

Prawn heads
5g paprika
Extra virgin olive oil
Rosemary
Thyme
Lemon zest
Fine sea salt

Preheated oven on 200°C.

In a frying pan sauté the prawn shells, season and add the herbs, paprika and the zest.

Roast in the oven for 15 minutes.

Transfer to a tray and dehydrate for 12 hours at 60°C.

Blend in a spice grinder and pass through a fine sieve.

Keep in an airtight container until needed.

## BURNT CUCUMBER, VERVEINE, MINT

12 x 1cm cubes of cucumber seeds
A few fresh leaves of verveine and mint

Char the cucumber with a blowtorch and, whilst still warm, vac pac with a few of the leaves of verveine and mint.

Refrigerate for at least 2 hours, until needed.

## BUTTERED TOAST ICE CREAM

6 slices granary bread, toasted dark but not burnt
80g unsalted butter
100g caster sugar
150g pasteurised egg yolk
1 litre full fat milk
30g whole skimmed milk powder

Toast the bread, butter well.

Whisk together the caster sugar and egg yolk.

Bring the milk and milk powder to the boil and pour onto the yolk mixture.

Return to the pan and slowly bring up to 80°C, stirring with a spatula.

Remove from the heat and pass through a fine sieve into a clean bowl.

Add the toast and leave to infuse for 45 minutes.

Pass through a fine sieve (a lot of the ice cream mix will have soaked into the toast, push this through a sieve with the back of a ladle).

Chill.

Churn in an ice cream machine as per the manufacturer's instructions.

# LANGOUSTINE, SMOKED EEL WHEY AND PISTACHIO

## LANGOUSTINE TARTARE

2 langoustine tails per person, peeled and deveined
A little fresh lemon juice
Extra virgin olive oil
Fine sea salt

Wash the peeled langoustine tails thoroughly in iced water and freeze for 24 hours.
Remove from the freezer and defrost in the fridge on a J-cloth to absorb any excess moisture.
Cut into small pieces and season with a little sea salt, lemon juice and extra virgin olive oil.

## SMOKED EEL WHEY

400g buttermilk
2 thyme sprigs
70g smoked eel trimmings
Fine sea salt

Bring the all the ingredients to the boil.
Remove from the heat and leave to infuse for 15 minutes.
Pass through a fine sieve and season.

## PISTACHIO OIL

90g shelled pistachios
150g pistachio oil
A few drops of fish sauce

Blend all the ingredients until smooth.
Pass through a fine sieve and store in the fridge until needed.

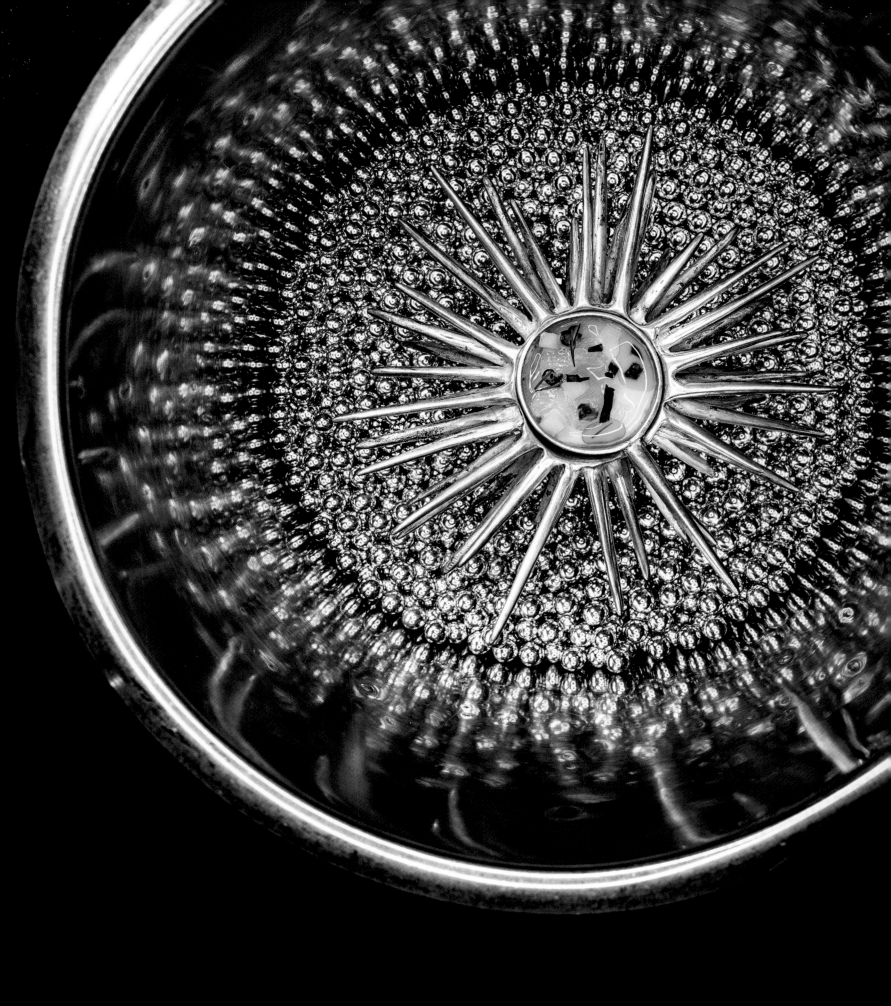

# RED MULLET, WALNUT, PARMESAN, ARTICHOKE AND PINK GRAPEFRUIT

## RED MULLET

4 red mullet (about 180g each)

Scale, fillet and pin bone the red mullet.
Season and lightly grill with a little olive oil and some sea salt, skin side up under a hot grill for 2 minutes.

## GRAPEFRUIT

1 pink grapefruit, segmented and cut into small pieces

## WALNUT AND PARMESAN PESTO

150g walnut halves
50g grated Parmesan
80g walnut oil
Seasoning

Blend all the ingredients in a food processor to a smooth paste.

## ARTICHOKES

4 violet artichokes
1 stick of celery, finely sliced
White of half a leek, finely sliced
1 carrot, finely diced
1 bayleaf
6 black peppercorns
2 garlic cloves, finely sliced
Juice of 1 lemon mixed with water
150g extra virgin olive oil
Seasoning

Remove the large outer leaves of the artichokes by breaking them off and with a small sharp knife cut off the smaller leaves.

Place in the lemon juice and water to stop browning.

Place in a pan with all the other ingredients, cover with water and gently simmer until tender (about 20 minutes).

Alternatively, cut the artichokes in half and place all the ingredients in a vac pac bag, seal and cook in a water bath set at 82°C for 18 minutes.

When cooked, plunge the unopened bags into an ice bath until cold.

# ORGANIC SALMON, BUDDHA'S HAND, PINK GRAPEFRUIT AND CHICKEN FAT MAYONNAISE

## SALMON

4 x 100g organic salmon fillet

Pin bone and skin the salmon, coat with a little extra virgin olive oil and season.

Cook on a plancha (or frying pan), when golden turn over cook for a further minute (or until three quarters cooked).

Remove from the heat and finish with a little fresh lemon juice, leave to finish cooking with the residual heat of the pan.

## BUDDHA'S HAND

1 Buddha's hand, sliced very thinly widthways
250g mirin (cooking saki)
250g rice wine vinegar

Bring the mirin and rice wine vinegar to the boil and reduce by one third.

Remove from the heat and add the Buddha's hand slices.

Cover and leave to cool.

The pickled Buddha's hand can be kept chilled in an airtight box for two weeks.

## PINK GRAPEFRUIT

1 pink grapefruit

Peel and segment the grapefruit, cut each segment into five small pieces and keep in its juice until needed.

## CHICKEN FAT MAYONNAISE

100g egg yolks
15g white balsamic or white wine vinegar
15g Dijon mustard
Large pinch of Maldon salt
15g cold water
200g warm, melted roast chicken fat
30g thyme, chives and chervil, finely chopped

Blend the egg yolks, mustard and vinegar together in a blender. Season.

Slowly add the warm chicken fat, then the cold water and lastly the herbs.

Check for seasoning and if not quite sharp enough add a few more drops of vinegar.

Chill until ready to use.

# SCALLOP PORRIDGE

### SCALLOPS

4 scallops per person
Small knob of butter
Fresh lemon juice

Pan-fry the lightly seasoned scallops in a hot pan until golden on one side, gently turn over and continue to cook for another minute.
Remove from the heat, add the butter and lemon juice and baste for 30 seconds.

### PARSLEY OIL

350g extra virgin olive oil
1 medium bunch of flat leaf parsley, large stalks removed

Plunge the parsley into boiling water for 30 seconds and refresh in ice water.
Squeeze all the water out and place in a food blender with the olive oil.
Turn on and blend on high for 1 minute.
Strain through a J-cloth lined sieve.
Keep in an airtight container until needed.

### PORRIDGE

150g heavily smoked bacon, finely diced (such as Alsace)
50g pinhead porridge oats
100g laverbread
250g water (to start)
20g smoked butter

In a small pan fry the smoked bacon and cook until coloured.
Add the water and deglaze the bottom of the pan.
Add the oats and turn the heat down, stirring until all the water has been absorbed and the oats are 70% cooked (about 5 minutes on a medium heat).
Add the laverbread and smoked butter, remove from the heat and stir to incorporate everything, check for seasoning.
The porridge should have the same loose texture as risotto (if a little firm you may need a little more water).
Check seasoning (both the laverbread and smoked bacon are naturally salty).

### TO SERVE

50 year-old balsamic vinegar to finish each plate

# SUCKLING PIG BELLY, SCALLOP, WATERMELON AND MEAD KETCHUP

### SUCKLING PIG

1 suckling pig belly, about 500g
2 bay leaves
10 black peppercorns

Cut the pork belly in two and vacuum seal them individually with one bayleaf and a few black peppercorns.
Cook at 75°C for 15 hours.
Remove from the bath, cool down and remove from the bag.
Remove the bones and the cartilage and press between two trays in the fridge overnight.
Cut into portions, rub a few drops of sunflower oil on the skin.
Roast for 10 minutes skin side down in a dry pan until you have good crackling. Keep warm.
Alternatively place in a deep tray and spoon over 350g duck fat, cover with foil and slowly bake in the oven at 140°C for 8 hours.

### ROAST PORK JUS

1kg chicken wings
1kg pork bones
500g leek, finely sliced
300g carrot, finely sliced
4 onions, finely sliced
500g Beaujolais or other light red wine
100g white balsamic vinegar
4 cloves
1 tablespoon sugar
2 oranges, juiced

Roast off the pork bones and chicken wings until golden brown with half of the onions, place in a large pan, add half the leeks and the carrot and fill with water, bring to the boil and reduce by 70%. Pass through a sieve.
In a smaller pan sweat off the remainder of the vegetables until very browned, add the sugar and caramelise, deglaze with the wine then the orange juice.
Then add the vinegar and cloves and reduce by half, add the stock and reduce until syrupy (about 350ml) strain, correct the seasoning and leave to one side.

### MEAD KETCHUP

400g pears, roughly chopped
120g caster sugar
150g white balsamic, white wine or cider vinegar
8g lemon juice
40g mead
2 teaspoons xanthan gum (optional)

Place all the ingredients except the xanthan in a pan and bring to the boil.
Turn down the heat to a simmer and cook the pears until soft (about 20 minutes).
Using a slotted spoon remove the pears and blend in a food processor until smooth adding some of the liquid until you reach the consistency of tomato ketchup.
If using, add the xanthan gum and blend for another 10 seconds.
Pass through a sieve, check the seasoning and store in a plastic bottle.

### GRILLED WATERMELON

Cut eight cubes of watermelon, removing any seeds, vacuum seal on the highest setting, cut open the bag and repeat this twice (this will remove any excess water from the melon, making it crunchy and giving it a firmer texture when grilled).
When ready to grill, remove from the bag, lightly season and drizzle with olive oil. Grill under a hot salamander for 3 minutes until just warm, reserve.

### SCALLOPS

Place 16 scallops on a dry cloth and season well.
Pan-fry in a hot pan with a little olive oil until golden brown, turn over and cook for a further 1 minute, remove from the heat, finish with freshly squeezed lemon and more fresh olive oil.
Remove from the pan and check seasoning.

### VEGETABLE GARNISH

4 leaves of cavolo nero cabbage
16 very thin slices of candy beetroot

Lightly blanche the cavolo nero, dress and season.
Lightly grill the beetroot for 30 seconds and season with fine sea salt and olive oil.
Warm the sauce at the last minute, check the seasoning and consistency and spoon over.

# SEA-CURED MACKEREL, CHARRED CUCUMBER SEEDS, PUFFED WILD RICE AND SMOKED HAY MAYONNAISE

## MACKEREL

500g sea water, boiled and chilled
200g white wine vinegar
100g caster sugar
2 mackerel, filleted and pin boned

Whisk the caster sugar and the vinegar together.
Completely cover the mackerel fillets in the cold seawater and leave for 35 minutes.
Drain, pat dry and cover with the vinegar solution and leave again for 35 minutes.
Drain and pat dry.
Lightly grill the mackerel fillets with a little olive oil.

## SMOKED HAY OIL

500g rapeseed, groundnut or sunflower oil
3 large handfuls of hay
1 large pan with a tight fitting lid

(This must be done outside).
Line the inside of the large pan with hay and put a smaller metal pan containing the oil on top.
Light the hay with a blowtorch and put the lid on.
This will extinguish the flames and the oil will absorb the smoke.
Do this three times.

## SMOKED HAY MAYONNAISE

100g egg yolks
1 teaspoon french mustard
500g smoked hay oil
Seasoning
1 dessert spoon white wine vinegar
1 dessert spoon water

In a food blender blitz the yolks, mustard and slowly add the oil, then all the other ingredients to taste.

## PUFFED WILD RICE

Heat a small frying pan with a quarter inch of olive oil until very hot.
Add a dessert spoon of wild rice and swirl the pan, the rice will start to pop.
Drain the rice through a small sieve and place on kitchen paper to dry.
Season.

## CHARRED CUCUMBER SEEDS

Cut four batons from the centre of the cucumber (keeping the rest for a different recipe).
Place on a tray, lightly blowtorch and drizzle with a few drops of Minus 8 maple verjus.

# WILD SEA BASS, LINSEED,
# WILD GARLIC AND SQUID INK

## SEA BASS

4 x 150g portions wild sea bass, scaled and pin boned
Maldon sea salt
50g butter
Juice of half a lemon

## LINSEED CRISP

160g linseeds
300g water
2g salt

Combine all the ingredients, and leave for 6–8 hours.
Once the seed is hydrated spread thinly on a Silpat mat and leave in a warm place to dry.
Break into small pieces.

## WILD GARLIC OIL

100g wild leaf garlic
300g extra virgin olive oil
Seasoning

Blend the ingredients for 1 minute on high speed in a food blender.
Pour the ingredients into a muslin-lined sieve and leave to drip (the puréed garlic can be used in pesto).
Store the oil in a small plastic sauce bottle until needed.

## BURNT AUBERGINE
## AND SQUID INK PURÉE

2 aubergines
8g of squid ink
200g extra virgin olive oil
A small amount of xanthan gum

Reheat the oven to 200°C.
Cut the aubergines in half lengthways and drizzle with extra virgin olive oil.
Season and roast in the oven for 25 minutes or until soft.
Remove from the oven and blowtorch until the skin is blistered.
Transfer everything to a food blender, add the squid ink, 100g extra virgin olive oil and a little cold water (enough to get the blender mixing).
If needed add a small amount of xanthan gum.
Season, pass through a sieve and chill until needed.

Pan-fry the sea bass skin side down in a little olive oil over a medium heat until golden brown, carefully turn over and cook for a further minute on the flesh side.
Remove from the heat, add the butter and baste for a further minute, add the lemon juice and carefully lift from the pan.
Alternatively, salt cure the portions for 20 minutes, wash well and pat dry, vac pac with a small amount of olive oil.
Cook at 55°C for 13 minutes.
Remove from the bag, pat dry with a clean J-cloth.
Crisp the skin.

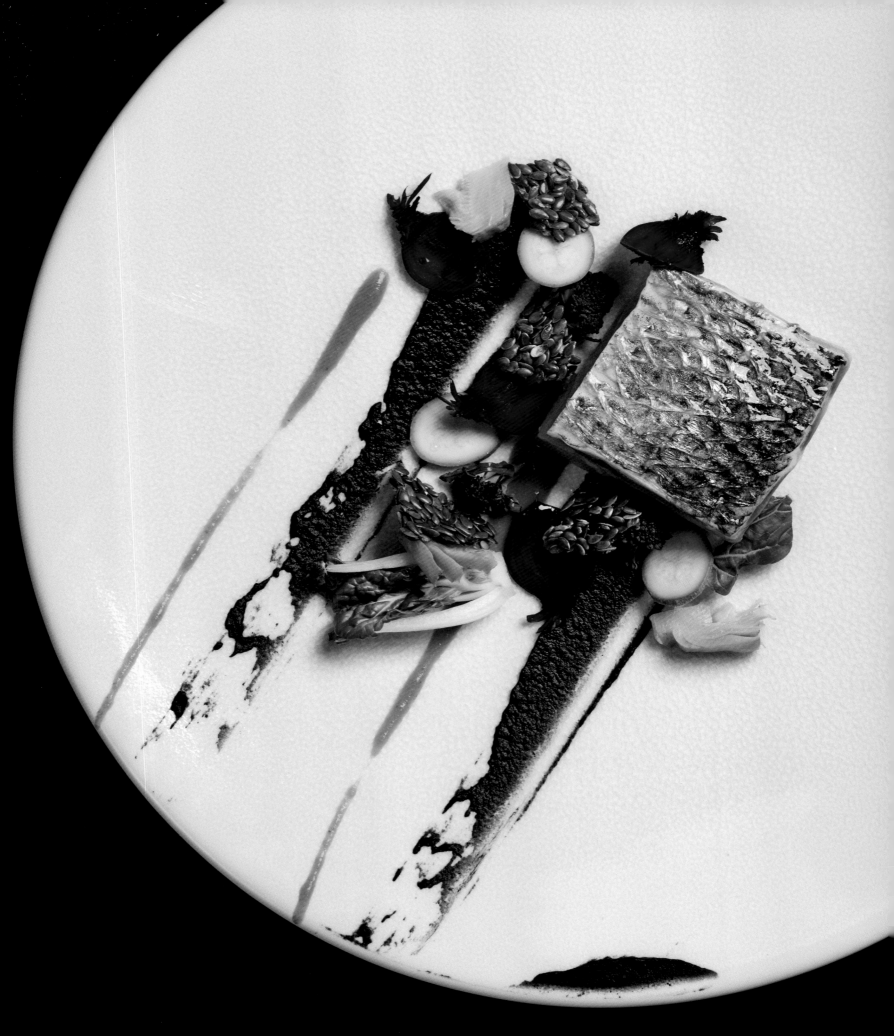

# SMOKED EEL, CHICKEN SKIN, BEER-PICKLED ONIONS AND BROWN SAUCE

## SMOKED EEL MOUSSE

200g smoked eel fillet
1 litre semi-skimmed milk
150g double cream
5 leaves of gelatine, soaked in cold water
3g Texturas Kappa
50g cold smoked butter
Smoked salt

Place the milk, cream, smoked eel and smoked butter in a saucepan and bring up to a simmer.

Turn the heat down and leave for 15 minutes (until the smoked eel has started to break up).

Add the Kappa and bring back up to a simmer (being careful not to boil over).

Transfer everything to a food blender, add the squeezed out gelatine and blend on medium.

Season with the smoked salt.

Pass through a sieve, pour into moulds and set in the fridge.

When serving use a warm knife to carefully unmould the eel mousse.

## CRISPY CHICKEN SKIN

Chicken skin from the breast
Seasoning

Preheat the oven to 150°C.

Remove all the excess lumps of fat from the underside of the skin by scraping with the side of a medium sized kitchen knife.

Lay the skin completely flat on a non-stick mat on a baking tray.

Lightly season the skin and place another non-stick mat and another baking tray on top (this will keep the skin flat and also squeeze the fat from the skin.

Place in the oven until golden brown (about 40 minutes).

Remove from the oven, remove the top tray and the top mat and leave to cool.

Store in an airtight box at room temperature for up to 3 days.

## BROWN SAUCE

1 onion, finely chopped
5 cloves
1 star anise
80g dried dates
65g soft dark brown sugar
70g black treacle
2 dessert spoons concentrated tamarind paste
325g tomatoes, chopped
450g malt vinegar
1 dessert spoon grain mustard
1 teaspoon ground ginger
1 dessert spoon ground allspice
Seasoning
Xanthan gum, as needed

Sweat the onions in a little oil, add all the other ingredients and slowly cook for 40 minutes. Allow to cool.

When just warm, transfer to a blender and purée until smooth (adding a small amount of xanthan gum powder if needed). The gum will slightly thicken the sauce.

Pass through a sieve and store in the fridge in a container with a tight-fitting lid or an airtight sauce bottle.

## BEER-PICKLED ONIONS

5 bunches of grelot onions (just the bulb part)
400g ale
180g honey
220g white balsamic or white wine vinegar
1 teaspoon fine sea salt
A few sprigs of rosemary and thyme

Cut the bulb onions in half.

Boil the ale, blanch in boiling salted water for 20 seconds with the honey, herbs and vinegar.

Leave to cool slightly and pour onto the dry onions.

Allow to stand for a few minutes then store in a sterilised jar or vac pac and leave for at least 24 hours before using.

# SMOKED HALIBUT, FIZZY GRAPES, HORSERADISH SNOW, PICKLED APPLE

## SMOKED HALIBUT

500g piece of wild atlantic halibut, skinned and boned
250g sea salt
150g caster sugar
5 juniper berries, crushed
A few sprigs of thyme
A few sprigs of rosemary
Small amount of whisky

Mix all the ingredients together except the whisky and cover the halibut, chill for 6 hours.

Wash well, pat dry and brush with the whisky, leave uncovered in the fridge for 8 hours to air dry.

On a tray, place in a smoker and cold smoke with oak chips for 6 hours.

Wrap in greaseproof paper, chill overnight.

Slice thinly just before serving.

## HORSERADISH SNOW

75g grated fresh horseradish
550g semi-skimmed milk
5g cornflour
Juice of half a lemon
Sea salt

Dilute the cornflour with a small amount of water.

Warm the milk and whisk in the cornflour, allow to thicken slightly and remove from the heat, add the grated horseradish and leave to infuse for 6 hours.

Strain through a fine sieve.

Check seasoning and add the lemon juice.

Pour into Pacojet containers and freeze.

Churn in the Pacojet for 10 seconds at a time, remove the 'snow' and store in an airtight box in the freezer.

Repeat until you have as much as you need.

Alternatively you can pour the horseradish milk into a plastic container and freeze, when solid scrape with a fork until you have fine crystals.

Store in the freezer until needed.

## FIZZY GRAPES

150g seedless grapes, cut in half
1 litre syphon gun with 2 $CO_2$ chargers

Place the grapes inside the soda syphon gun, screw on the lid and charge with the $CO_2$ chargers, agitating slightly but don't shake too hard as it will damage the grapes.

Chill for at least 4 hours.

When needed, place a cloth over the nozzle and gently release the gas.

*Very important: release the gas before you unscrew the top.*

## PICKLED GRANNY SMITH

2 Granny Smith apples
200g white vinegar
170g caster sugar
3 sprigs of thyme
Juice of 1 lemon

Peel and cut the apples into 5mm dice.

Bring the vinegar, sugar, lemon juice and thyme to the boil.

Remove from the heat and chill.

When cold add the apples and leave refrigerated for at least 6 hours before use.

# SMOKED SALMON, WAKAMOMO BABY PEACHES, TERIYAKI AND LOTUS ROOT

### SALMON

Organic salmon, skinned and cut into 5cm cubes
(1 per person)
200g fine sea salt
200g caster sugar
A few sprigs of rosemary
Small amount of whisky

Mix the sugar, salt and rosemary together and cover the salmon, chill for 2 hours.
Rinse off under cold water and pat dry.
Leave uncovered in the fridge for 3 hours to dry the surface.
Brush the salmon with the whisky and cold smoke with oak chips for 6 hours.
Leave covered in greaseproof paper overnight in the fridge (this will make the flavour a little mellower).

### WAKAMOMO BABY PEACHES

4 Wakamomo baby peaches, sliced very thinly

### TERIYAKI

100g caster sugar
65g glucose
250g mirin
110g dark soy sauce
8g bonito flakes
50g grated fresh ginger

Make a dark caramel with the caster sugar and the glucose.
Carefully and slowly add the liquid ingredients and gently whisk to dissolve the caramel.
Bring to a simmer.
Add the bonito and the fresh ginger.
Simmer for 20 minutes.
Strain.
If a little too sweet balance it with more rice wine vinegar.

### LOTUS ROOT

1 medium sized lotus root
(available online or from Asian supermarkets)
150g rice wine vinegar
100g caster sugar

Peel the lotus root and slice thinly on a mandolin.
Bring the vinegar and sugar to the boil and pour on the thinly sliced lotus root.
Leave to cool and chill until needed.

# HOME SMOKED SEA BASS
# IN ITS NATURAL SURROUNDINGS

*We serve this on rocks from the local beach that have been
frozen to -18°C. It is best eaten with your hands.*

## SEA BASS

1 x 3kg sea bass, scaled, filleted and pin boned
250g sea salt
150g caster sugar
5 juniper berries, crushed
A few sprigs of thyme
A few sprigs of rosemary
Small amount of whisky

Mix all the ingredients together except the whisky
and cover the fillets of sea bass, chill for 4 hours.

Wash well, pat dry and brush with the whisky.

Leave uncovered in the fridge for
4 hours to air dry on a tray.

Place in a smoker and cold smoke
with oak chips for 6 hours.

Wrap in greaseproof paper
and chill overnight.

Slice thinly.

## PICKLED SEAWEED

100g seaweed (nori, dulce or sea
lettuce pickle best)
200g white wine vinegar
100g caster sugar

Bring the vinegar and caster sugar to the
boil, remove from the heat, leave for
1 minute then pour onto the seaweed.
Chill until needed, pickled seaweed will
keep for several weeks chilled.

## LAVERBREAD EMULSION

105g egg yolks
1 teaspoon french mustard
500g of vegetable or groundnut oil
Seasoning
50g laverbread (half a small tin)
1 dessert spoon white wine vinegar
1 teaspoon water

In a food blender blitz the yolks and
mustard, slowly add the oil, then all the
other ingredients to taste.

## BEACH HERBS

sea aster, sea purslane, samphire,
oyster leaf, sea fennel

# SQUID, BEACH HERBS, PICKLED REDCURRANTS AND COFFEE

## BABY SQUID

4 x 150g baby squid
A little fresh lemon juice
Extra virgin olive oil
Seasoning

Clean the squid, slice lengthways and score in a criss cross pattern on the inside of the flesh.
Wash the tentacles, discard the beak, cut in two.
Squid this size only takes seconds to cook.
Drizzle a hot pan with good olive oil, season the squid and sear for 15 seconds on each side.
Remove from the heat and finish with a little lemon juice.

## BEACH HERBS

sea fennel
sea aster
samphire

## PICKLED REDCURRANTS

200g white wine vinegar
200g caster sugar
Thyme leaves
150g redcurrants, stalks removed

Bring the white wine vinegar and caster sugar to the boil, add the thyme, remove from the heat and leave to cool for 30 minutes.
When lukewarm pour onto the redcurrants.
Chill until needed.

## COFFEE OIL

200g extra virgin olive oil
40g good quality coffee beans
3 large sprigs of thyme

Warm all the ingredients to 60°C, keep warm for an hour, pass through a sieve.
Store in a plastic bottle until needed.

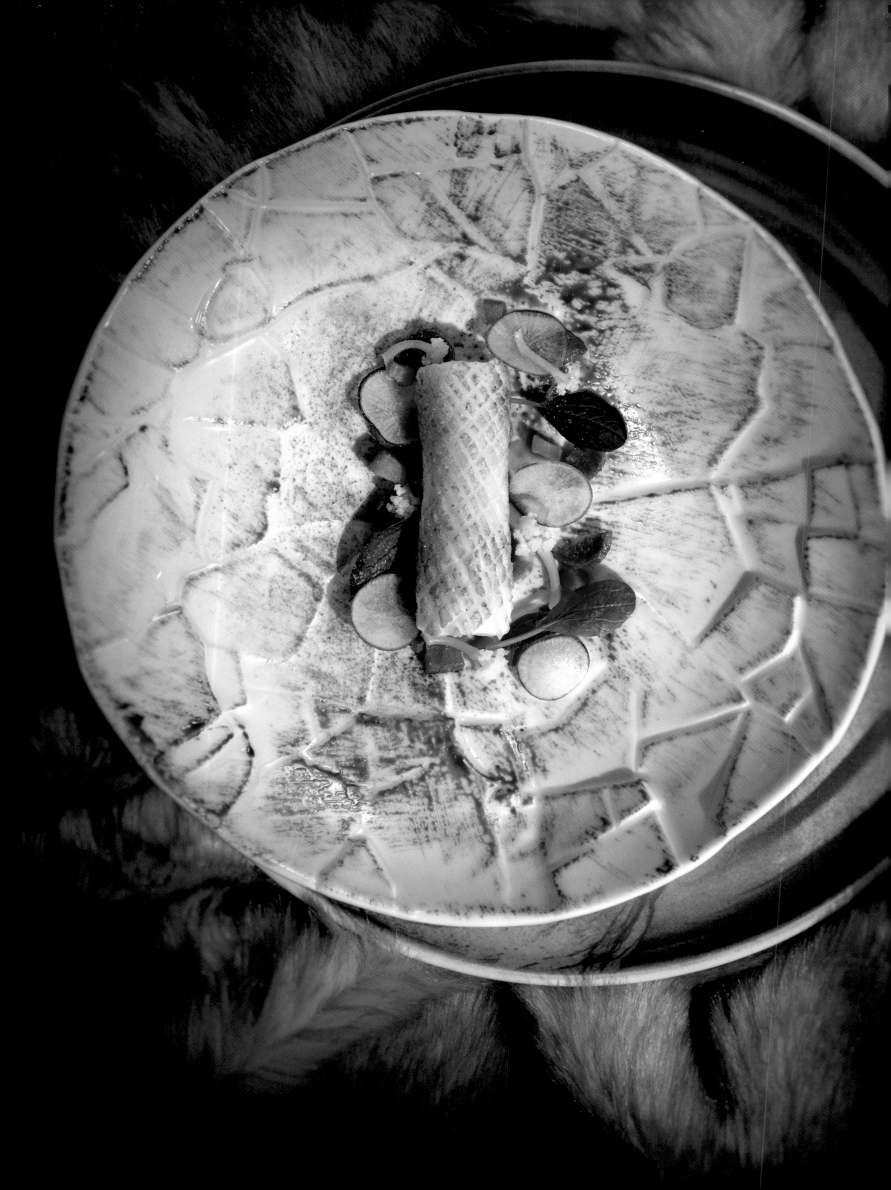

# BABY SQUID, MERGUEZ, GOOSEBERRY, MAPLE VERJUS AND BLACK GARLIC

### BABY SQUID

3 x 150g baby squid
A little fresh lemon juice
Extra virgin olive oil
Seasoning

Clean the squid, slice lengthways and score in a criss cross pattern on the inside of the flesh.
Wash the tentacles, discard the beak, cut in two.
Squid this size only takes seconds to cook.
Drizzle a hot pan with good olive oil, season the squid and sear for 15 seconds on each side.
Remove from the heat and finish with a little lemon juice.

### MERGUEZ

2 medium spiced merguez sausages

Blanch the sausages in simmering water for 2 minutes.
Remove and chill.
Slice very thinly.
Crisp the thin slices under a grill with a little olive oil just before serving.

### GOOSEBERRY PURÉE

150g gooseberries
70g sugar
50g water
1 teaspoon of xanthan gum
A few drops of Minus 8 maple verjus

Put the gooseberries, sugar and water in a small saucepan and bring to the boil.
Remove from the heat and leave to cool slightly.
Transfer to a blender and blend until smooth.
Add the xanthan.
Check for seasoning and add a little verjus to correct the acidity.
Pass through a sieve and store in a plastic bottle until needed.

### BLACK GARLIC

75g gem lettuce
3 dried apricots, diced
10g unsalted butter, melted
30g black garlic
70g vegetable stock
Small pinch xanthan gum
10g toasted sesame oil
3 good size thyme sprigs
Maldon sea salt

Sauté the lettuce in a pan, season and baste with butter until dark.
Add all the other ingredients except the xanthan and simmer for 10 minutes.
Remove the thyme.
Transfer to a blender and blend until smooth add the xanthan.
Pass through a sieve and check for seasoning.

# THE SEA

*This dish has always been massively popular, the best part is that it is so versatile; you can change the ingredients to suit your personal taste.*

## CRAB

1 brown cock crab, about 1kg
(those from the west country are best)
A little lemon juice

Plunge the crab into heavily salted boiling water, cook for 9 minutes.
Refresh in cold water and drain.
Crack the claws and the top joint of the smaller legs, reserving the meat in the body for another recipe.
Pick through the white meat, checking for pieces of shell.
Season with a little lemon juice, salt and a few drops of olive oil.
Keep chilled until needed.

## MUSSELS

200g mussels, cleaned and bearded
100g dry white wine
1 shallot, peeled and finely diced
A little butter

Melt the butter in a medium sized pan on a low heat, add the shallot and sweat for a minute without colour.
Add the wine, turn up the heat and bring to the boil.
Add the mussels, put the lid on and shake the pan.
Steam the mussels until they are open, discarding any that stay closed.
Refresh under cold water and pick from the shells.

## MUSSEL SHELLS

100g pasta flour
50g water
10g squid ink
2g fine sea salt
20 mussel shell halves, emptied, cleaned and completely dried

Make a smooth black dough from the first four ingredients, cover with cling film and leave to rest in the fridge for at least 4 hours.
Oil the mussel shells liberally.
Roll the dough through a pasta machine.
Using two mussel shells that fit tightly together, press the dough onto the shells, making sure it overlaps the lips of the shells.
Fry at 180°C for a few minutes.
*(The shells will need a little pressure to hold them together for the first minute or so of cooking; we use the tips of plating tweezers, but be extremely careful not to burn yourself).*

## OCTOPUS

1 mediterranean octopus
250g dry white wine
Enough water to cover
Seasoning

In a large pan cover the octopus with the wine and water, season well.
Bring up to the boil, turn down the heat and simmer for 4-5 hours (or until tender).
When cooked, cool slightly in the water and remove.
When cold enough to handle, remove the suckers and outside membrane, wash in cold water.
Chill until needed.

*continued...*

## LOBSTER

1 x 750g lobster

Cook the lobster in boiling salted water for 7 minutes, refresh in an ice water bath, drain and chill.
Crack the shells and remove the flesh.

## SEA WATER

1 litre of water
1 small bulb of fennel, finely sliced
1 small onion, finely sliced
1 small piece of white of leek
1 bay leaf
10 black peppercorns
100g fresh seaweed (dulce or sea lettuce work best)
1 lemon in thin slices
5g lecithin

Place all the ingredients except the lemon and the lecithin in a pan and bring to the boil.
Turn down the heat and simmer for 15 minutes.
Remove from the heat and add the lemon.
Cover with cling film and leave to infuse for 2 hours.
Pass through a fine sieve, chill.
When needed, remove from the fridge, add the lecithin and blend with an electric hand blender until dissolved.
Run the blender over the surface of the liquid until a light foam appears (the lecithin will stabilise the foam).
Carefully gather foam off the surface.

## CLAMS

200g clams, rinsed under cold running water
100g dry white wine
1 shallot, peeled and finely diced
A little butter

Melt the butter in a medium pan on a low heat, add the shallot and sweat for a minute without colour.
Add the wine, turn up the heat and bring to the boil.
Add the clams, put the lid on and shake the pan.
Steam the clams until they are open.
Discard any that stay closed.
Refresh under cold water and pick from the shells.

## PICKLED SEAWEED

250g white wine vinegar
250g caster sugar
200g sea lettuce

Boil the vinegar and sugar, remove from the heat and leave for 10 minutes.
When lukewarm, pour onto the sea lettuce and leave refrigerated for at least 24 hours before use.

## FRESH BEACH HERBS

Sea aster, Sea purslane, Samphire

## SEA LETTUCE POWDER

200g sea lettuce

Place the sea lettuce on a lined dehydrator tray and dry at 52°C until crispy (usually around 6 hours).
Blend and pass through a sieve.
The sea lettuce powder will keep for a month in an airtight box at room temperature.

# SQUID, REDCURRANT, KOHLRABI, PEA AND PINE

### BABY SQUID

3 x 150g baby squid
A little fresh lemon juice
Extra virgin olive oil
Seasoning

Clean the squid, slice lengthways and score in a criss cross pattern on the inside of the flesh.

Wash the tentacles, discard the beak, cut in two.

Squid this size only takes seconds to cook.

Drizzle a hot pan with good olive oil, season the squid and sear for 15 seconds on each side.

Remove from the heat and finish with a little lemon juice.

### PICKLED REDCURRANTS

300g white wine vinegar
200g caster sugar
A few sprigs of thyme
300g redcurrants, stalks removed

Boil the sugar, vinegar and thyme and leave to cool.

When cold add to the redcurrants and chill for at least 24 hours before use.

### KOHLRABI

12 thin slices of kohlrabi
Olive oil
Seasoning

Drizzle a little olive oil over the kohlrabi and cook on a plancha or griddle for 20 seconds each side, season.

### PEA POWDER

500g frozen peas

Blanch the frozen peas in boiling water for 30 seconds, refresh in iced water and drain.

Transfer to a lined dehydrator tray and dry on 40°C until completely dry (about 8 hours).

Blend in a spice grinder and pass through a sieve.

Keep ambient in an airtight box.

### PINE OIL

2 handfuls of young pine shoots (normal green pine needles will also make a good oil)
300g extra virgin olive oil

Blend the two ingredients in a food processor for 45 seconds on high speed.

Strain through a muslin-lined sieve.

Store the oil in the refrigerator until use.

(This oil will keep chilled for 4 weeks).

# WILD SEA TROUT, HAZELNUT,
# 63°C YOLK, HISPI, ASH AND BEECH

## WILD SEA TROUT

100g Wild sea trout filleted and pin boned (per person)
Hispi cabbage leaves
Fresh lemon juice
Fine sea salt

Blanch the hispi leaves in boiling salted water, refresh in iced water and drain them on a J-cloth.
Drizzle with a little extra virgin olive oil, season and crisp under a low grill or a plancha.

## HAZELNUT PESTO

350g hazelnuts, husks removed
100g grated Parmesan
150g hazelnut oil
1 dessert spoon fresh thyme, chopped
Fine sea salt

Blend all the ingredients to a fine paste, season and store in an airtight container in the fridge until needed.

## ASH

1 bunch of dill
The green skin of 1 cucumber
The outer leaves of 2 leeks

Preheat the oven to 160°C.
On a dry heat (such as a barbecue or griddle pan), char all of the ingredients until black.
Place on a tray and dry in the oven until crispy and dry.
Remove from the oven and leave to cool.
Blend in a food processor and pass through a sieve.
Store in an airtight box at room temperature.

## BEECH LEAF OIL

150g young beech leaves
100g flat leaf parsley
500g pommice oil

Blend everything in a Thermomix for 7 minutes, strain through a J-cloth.
Store in a bottle, chilled until needed.

## 63°C EGG YOLK

1 medium sized free range egg per person

Set a water bath to 63°C
Carefully lower the eggs into the water bath and cook in their shells for 65 minutes.
Alternatively you could use a poached egg.

## TO SERVE

Season the wild sea trout fillets, drizzle with a little extra virgin olive oil and cook skin side down on a plancha (or under a grill), turning over when the skin is golden.
Finish with a little fresh olive oil and lemon juice.
Carefully remove the eggs with a slotted spoon from the water bath.
Crack them onto a J-cloth (if you wish you can use the whole egg, but for this dish we prefer to use just the yolk).
Using a spoon gently push away the white.
Season.

# WILD ATLANTIC HALIBUT, BURNT AUBERGINE, ROASTED PEPPERS, CHORIZO AND SOUR APRICOT

## WILD ATLANTIC HALIBUT

4 x 150g portions of wild Atlantic halibut,
2cm in thickness

Fine sea salt, to cure

Caster sugar, to cure

A little extra virgin olive oil

Lemon juice, to serve

Powdered dried sea lettuce, to serve

Cure the halibut in equal quantities of salt and
sugar for 20 minutes.

Wash well in iced water and pat dry with a
clean J-cloth.

Vac pac with a little olive oil and cook in a
water bath for 18 minutes at 53°C.

Remove from the bath and cut open the
halibut pouch.

Finish with a little olive oil, fresh lemon juice
and powdered dried sea lettuce.

## BURNT AUBERGINE PURÉE

3 aubergines
150g extra virgin olive oil
Fine sea salt
1 teaspoon xanthan gum
A little water

Preheat oven to 190°C.

Cut the aubergines lengthways and place on a stainless steel tray.

Drizzle over the olive oil and roast for 15 minutes.

Turn the aubergines over and roast for a further 10 minutes.

Remove from the oven and blowtorch all over until black and blistered.

Transfer to a food blender with any juices and oil from the roasting tray and the xanthan gum.

Season and add just enough water to blend until smooth.

Pass through a sieve and chill until needed.

## ROAST PEPPERS

2 red peppers
A little extra virgin olive oil
Fine sea salt

Preheat the oven to 200°C.

In an ovenproof dish, roast the peppers for 10 minutes (just until they start to soften).

Remove from the oven and blowtorch the skin until black and blistered.

Cling film the peppers in a container and chill (the heat from the peppers will steam their skins off, making them easier to peel).

When cold, peel the peppers and cut to the desired shape and size.

Season with a little fine sea salt and dress with a little extra virgin olive oil.

*continued…*

*Wild Atlantic Halibut, Burnt Aubergine, Chorizo and Sour Apricot Continued...*

## BABY ARTICHOKES

4 violet artichokes
1 celery stick, finely sliced
Half the white of a leek, finely sliced
1 carrot, finely diced
1 bay leaf
6 black peppercorns
2 garlic cloves, finely sliced
Juice of 1 lemon mixed with cold water
150g extra virgin olive oil
Seasoning

Remove the large outer leaves of the artichokes by breaking them off.
With a small sharp knife, peel the smaller leaves.
Add the artichokes to the lemon water to stop them browning.
Place in a pan with all the other ingredients, cover with water and gently simmer until tender (about 20 minutes).

Alternatively, peel the artichokes and cut in half.
Place all the ingredients in a vac pac bag.
Seal and cook in a water bath at 82°C for 18 minutes.
When ready, plunge the unopened bags into an ice bath until cold.

## SOUR APRICOT PURÉE

250g dried apricots
100g white wine vinegar
1 teaspoon xanthan gum

Place the dried apricots in a saucepan, add the vinegar and enough water to cover.
Bring to the boil, turn down to a simmer and cook until soft (about 25 minutes).
Remove from the heat and leave to stand for 15 minutes.
Transfer to a food blender and add enough of the poaching liquor to blend.
Add the xanthan gum and blend until smooth.
Pass through a sieve and chill until needed.

## TO SERVE, PER PERSON

5 slices of sweet chorizo, warmed with a little extra virgin olive oil just before serving.
3 thin slices of uncooked candy beetroot, seasoned.
4 thin slices of uncooked yellow beetroot, seasoned.
50 year-old balsamic vinegar.

# WHISKY-SMOKED WILD SEA TROUT

1 whole sea trout, about 1.5kg

300g sea salt

150g caster sugar

A few sprigs of thyme

15g dried camomile flowers

100g Scottish single malt whisky

A pepper mill filled with black peppercorns

21 oak whisky barrel biscuits for a cold smoker

Fillet and pin-bone the wild sea trout.

Mix together the salt, sugar, thyme and camomile flowers.

In a clean plastic container, cover the sea trout fillets with the mix and leave in the fridge for 3 hours.

Wash the fillets thoroughly in iced water and pat dry.

Using a pastry brush, paint the flesh of the trout with the whisky and a few twists of black pepper from the mill.

Leave to dry overnight in the fridge.

The next day, cold-smoke the sea trout fillets with oak whisky barrel chips for 7 hours.

Remove from the smoker, wrap in greaseproof paper and chill overnight.

Slice thinly when cold.

# MONKFISH, JAPANESE ARTICHOKES, PONZU SAUCE AND NASTURTIUM ROOT

## MONKFISH

4 x 150g thick pieces of monkfish
Fine sea salt, to cure
Sugar, to cure

Skin and remove any membrane from the monkfish tail and cut into portions.
Salt cure with equal quantities of fine sea salt and sugar.
Leave for 20 minutes.
Wash in ice water and pat dry.
Seal in a vac pac bag with a little extra virgin olive oil.
Cook in a water bath set to 55°C for 19 minutes.
(Alternatively, after patting the fish dry, pan-fry in good olive oil until golden each side).

## PICKLED JAPANESE ARTICHOKES

150g Japanese artichokes
200g rice vinegar
100g white wine vinegar
150g caster sugar

Clean the Japanese artichokes under running water, removing any dirt or root fibres.
Place the two vinegars and the sugar in a pan.
Bring to the boil, remove from the heat and leave to cool.
When cold pour onto the artichokes and leave for 24 hours before use.
Store in an airtight box in the fridge.
Alternatively, pour the cold pickling liquor in a bag with the artichokes in a vac pac bag and seal on full vacuum.

## PINEAPPLE

1 pineapple
3 cloves
5 allspice grains
1 star anise

Set a water bath to 48°C.
Peel the pineapple and cut lengthways into quarters.
Place in a vac pac bag with the spices and seal on 100% vacuum.
Cook in the water bath at 48°C for 3 hours.
Chill in an ice bath.
When cold cut to required shape and size.

## PONZU SAUCE

100g light soy sauce
100g dark soy sauce
35g fresh yuzu juice
250g rice wine vinegar
200g mirin
100g fresh ginger, finely chopped
100g sunflower oil
20g fresh coriander leaf
1 teaspoon xanthan gum

In a food processor, blend all the ingredients except the xanthan until smooth and well incorporated.
Thicken with a little xanthan gum and pass through a sieve.
When serving, bring the sauce up to a gentle simmer (not a boil, as it will split).

*continued…*

## ROAST PEPPERS

2 red peppers
A little extra virgin olive oil
Fine sea salt

Preheat oven to 200°C.
In an ovenproof dish, roast the peppers for 10 minutes (just until they start to soften).
Remove from the oven and blowtorch the skin until black and blistered.
While warm, place in a bowl and cover with cling film (this will help steam the skins off).
When cool, scrape the skins and seeds off the peppers.
When cold peel the peppers and cut to the desired shape and size.
Season with a little fine sea salt and dress with a little toasted sesame oil.

## NASTURTIUM ROOT

1 medium nasturtium root
250g mirin (cooking saki)
250g rice wine vinegar

Wash the nasturtium root well, pat dry and slice very thinly on a mandolin.
Bring the mirin and rice wine vinegar to the boil and reduce by one third.
Remove from the heat and add the thin slices of nasturtium root.
Cover and leave to cool.

## PUFFED WILD RICE

Heat a quarter of an inch of olive oil in a small frying pan until very hot.
Add a dessert spoon of wild rice and swirl the pan.
The rice will start to pop.
Drain the rice through a small sieve and place on kitchen paper to dry.
Season.

## PAK CHOI

16 small leaves from baby pak choi, lightly sautéed in a little sesame oil for 20 seconds.

# OCTOPUS, BLOOD ORANGE, CAMPARI AND FENNEL

## OCTOPUS

1 mediterranean octopus
250g dry white wine
Water as needed
Seasoning

In a large pan cover the octopus with the wine and water, season well.
Bring up to the boil, turn down the heat and simmer until tender (about 4 or 5 hours).
When cooked, cool slightly in the water, then remove.
When cold enough to handle, remove the suckers and outside membrane.
Wash under cold water and refrigerate for 2 hours.
Slice thinly (this will keep in the fridge for 3 days).
When serving dress with a little fresh lemon and extra virgin olive oil, and season.

## BLOOD ORANGE JAM

250g blood orange juice
250g caster sugar
750g blood oranges
125g extra virgin olive oil
1 teaspoon xanthan gum

Boil the juice and sugar and leave to cool.
Strain.
Pierce the oranges and boil them in water.
Change the water and repeat this three times.
Cut into quarters, remove all pips and cook further in the juice.
Blend in the thermomix and add the olive oil.
Slowly add the xanthan until the right consistency is obtained.

## CAMPARI ROCKS

Half a bottle of Campari

Pour the campari into a plastic container and leave to air dry somewhere warm.
The ambient temperature of the room will determine on how long the Campari will take to dry.
Once the campari has dried enough you will be able to break it up into small rocks (this will be very bitter so a little goes a long way).

## PICKLED FENNEL

250g white wine vinegar
250g caster sugar
A few sprigs of thyme
10 black peppercorns
1 bayleaf
1 head of fennel, thinly sliced

Bring all the ingredients except the fennel up to the boil.
Put the thinly sliced fennel in a bowl and pour on the pickling liquor.
Leave to cool.
Stored in an airtight container in the fridge, this will keep for up to 3 weeks.

# SKREI COD, WILD GARLIC, PICKLED SHIMEJI MUSHROOMS AND HAZELNUT OIL

*Skrei cod is a winter cod found in the north Norwegian waters. The Skrei feeds on shrimp, squid and mackerel. It is in season from January to March.*

### SKREI COD

4 x 150g thick pieces of skrei cod
Sea salt, for curing
Sugar, for curing
Extra virgin olive oil

Set a water bath to 55°C.
Skin and pin bone the cod portions.
Salt cure with equal quantities of fine sea salt and sugar.
Leave for 20 minutes.
Wash in ice water and pat dry.
Seal in a vac pac bag with a little extra virgin olive oil.
Cook in the water bath at 55°C for 19 minutes.
(Alternatively, after patting the fish dry, pan-fry in good olive oil until golden each side).

### BABY LEEKS

8 x baby leeks
A little hazelnut oil

Trim and wash the baby leeks in cold water.
Blanch in boiling salted water for 45 seconds.
Refresh in iced water.
Remove any of the tougher outer layers.
Season and warm through with a little hazelnut oil.

### PICKLED WILD GARLIC

300g white balsamic vinegar
150g caster sugar
Wild garlic leaves

Bring both ingredients to the boil, remove from the heat and leave to cool.
When cold pour on the wild garlic leaves.
Store in a sealed vac pac bag (alternatively in an airtight container in the fridge).

### WILD GARLIC, HAZELNUT AND PEA PURÉE

200g petits pois
12 pickled wild garlic leaves
100g hazelnut oil
Fine sea salt
1 teaspoon xanthan gum

In boiling salted water, blanch the peas for 30 seconds.
Drain the peas, reserving some of the water.
Transfer the peas to a blender.
Add the pickled garlic leaves and a little of the blanching water.
Blend until smooth.
Drizzle in the hazelnut oil and add the xanthan.
Check the seasoning and pass through a fine sieve.

### PICKLED SHIMEJI MUSHROOMS

150g white wine vinegar
100g caster sugar
2 large thyme sprigs
100g white shimeji mushrooms

Bring the vinegar, sugar and thyme to the boil.
Remove from the heat and leave to cool.
Remove the thyme and add the mushrooms.
Leave for at least 24 hours before use.

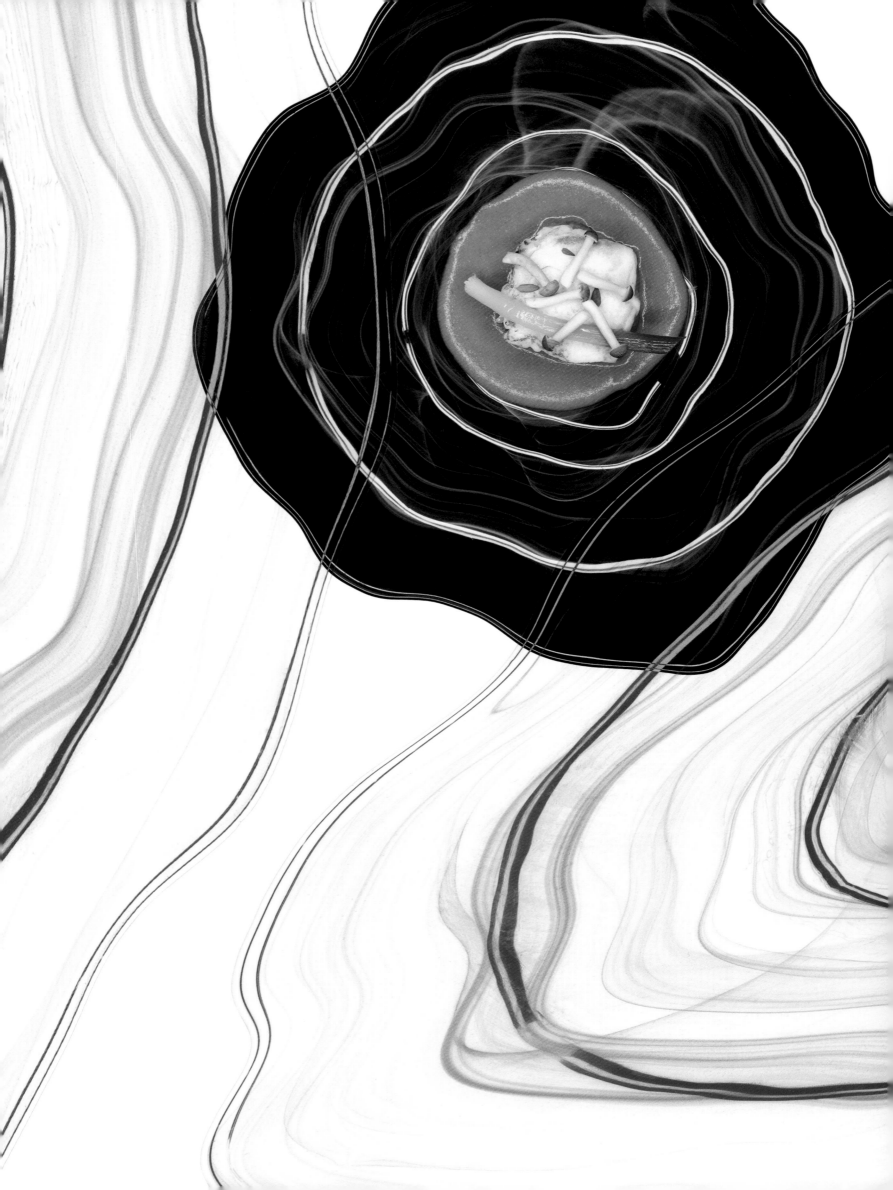

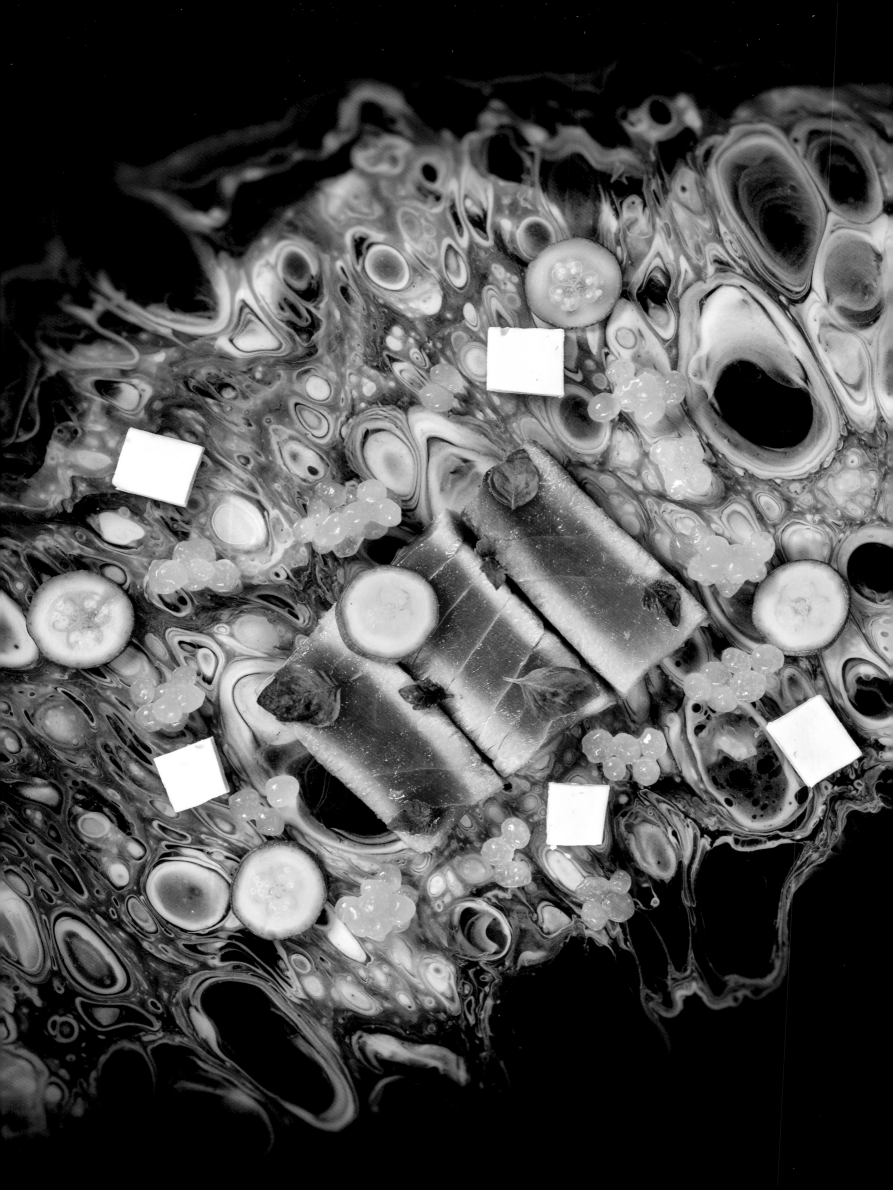

# TUNA, FETA, MELON, COURGETTE

## MELON CAVIAR

500g melon juice
(any other freshly squeezed juice will work with this recipe)
3.5g Texturas algin

Peel and de-seed the melon, cut into a large pieces and blend in a food processor until smooth.

Pass through a sieve.

Using a hand blender, incorporate 3.5g of Algin for every 500g of melon juice.

Blend until smooth and pass through a sieve.

Seal the juice in a vac pac bag to remove all bubbles and store in the fridge.

Using a pipette (or caviar box) dispense small caviar sized drops of juice into the calcic bath.

Leave for 1 minute.

Using a small conical strainer, remove the melon drops from the calcic bath and rinse gently under cold water.

Store in the fridge until needed.

The melon caviar will keep for up to 2 days.

## TUNA

120g sashimi grade tuna, sliced 1cm thick
Fine sea salt
A little fresh lemon juice

Season the tuna with the salt.

On a hot griddle or plancha, sear the tuna for 20 seconds each side and finish with fresh lemon juice.

Cut into three pieces.

## HALF-DRIED COURGETTE

3 medium courgettes

Peel the courgettes and lay on a lined dehydrator tray set to 40°C.

Dry until half the size (about 5 hours).

Store chilled in an airtight box until needed.

## FETA

5 small cubes of barrel-aged feta per person

Dress with a little extra virgin olive oil (the feta will already be salty enough).

## TO SERVE THE COURGETTES

3 thin slices of half-dried courgette per person
Extra virgin olive oil
Fine sea salt

Season the courgette slices and drizzle with a little extra virgin olive oil.

Cook on a tray under a hot grill for 45 seconds.

## CALCIC BATH

1 litre water
5g Texturas Calcic

In a shallow plastic container, dissolve the calcic in the water and keep it in the fridge.

# TURBOT CHAR SIU, PAK CHOI, MUSHROOM FRIED RICE

### TURBOT

150g turbot fillet, skin removed
Fine sea salt
Extra virgin olive oil
Fresh lemon juice

Season the turbot and drizzle with a little extra virgin olive oil.
Cook in either a hot pan or on a plancha until golden, turn the turbot over and cook for another 30 seconds.
Remove from the heat and finish with a little fresh lemon juice and more olive oil.
Leave to cook in the residual heat of the pan for 1 minute.

### CHAR SIU SAUCE

215g light soy sauce
100g dark soy sauce
230g hoisin sauce
260g fermented bean curd, including the chilli oil it is preserved in (this should be one small jar with the oil)
37g Chinese five spice
360g honey
180g rice wine vinegar
2g xanthan gum (optional)

Place all the ingredients into a food processor and blend until smooth, including the xanthan gum, if using.
Pass through a sieve.

### PAK CHOI

Pak choi
Toasted sesame oil
Fine sea salt

Cut the root off the pak choi and separate the leaves.
Wash thoroughly and drain well.
Sauté the leaves in a little toasted sesame oil until soft.
Season with fine sea salt.

### PUFFED WILD RICE

1 dessert spoon of wild rice
Olive oil

Heat a small frying pan with a quarter of an inch of olive oil until very hot.
Add the wild rice and swirl the pan; the rice will start to pop.
Drain the rice through a small sieve removing the excess oil and place on kitchen paper to dry.
Season with fine sea salt and a little cep powder.

### CEP POWDER

Sliced cep mushrooms

Place the mushrooms on a lined dehydrator tray and dry on 40°C until crispy.
Blend in a spice/coffee grinder until powdered.
Pass through a sieve.
Store at room temperature in an airtight box.

### SLICED RAW BUTTON MUSHROOM

Raw button mushrooms
Olive oil
Fine sea salt

Holding the stalk, slice the mushrooms very thinly on a mandolin.
Dress with a little olive oil and season with a few grains of fine sea salt.
Lay the slices overlapping on the cooked turbot and dust with a little cep powder.

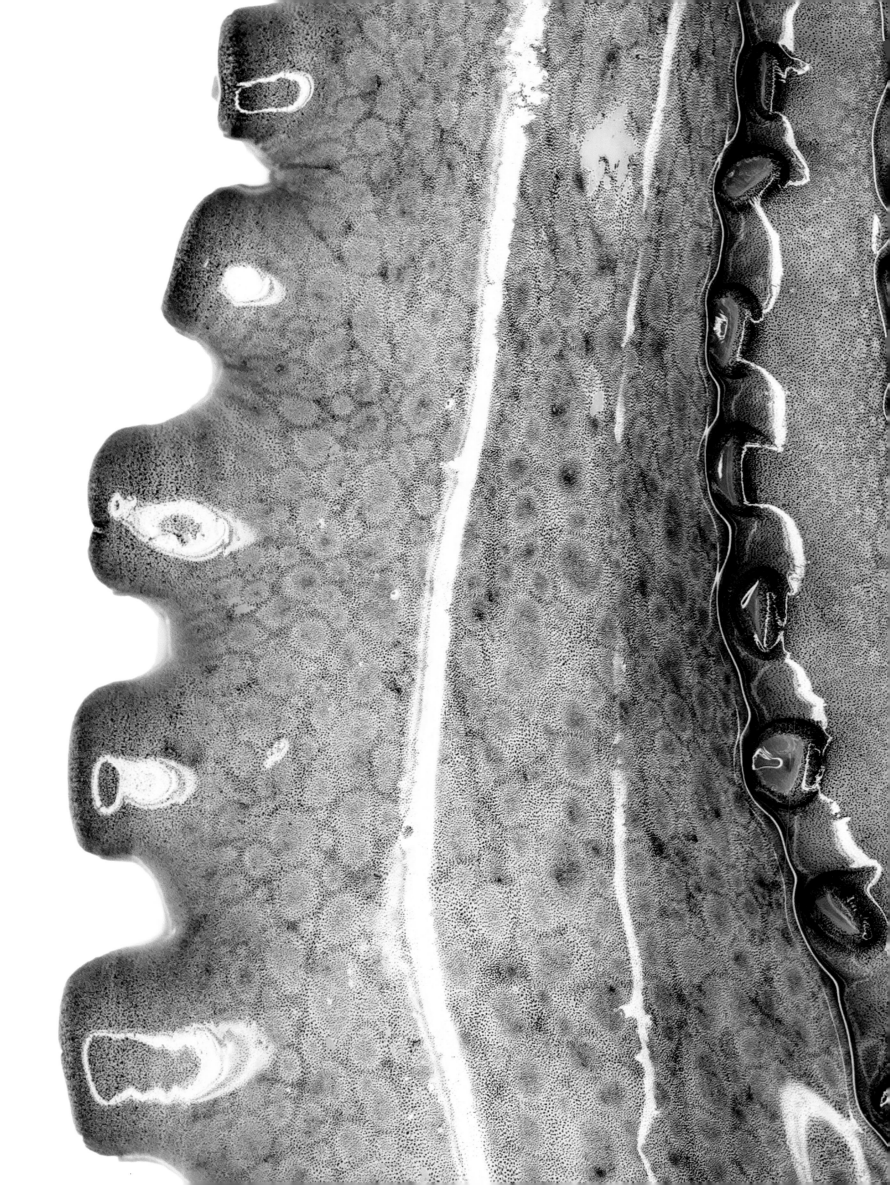

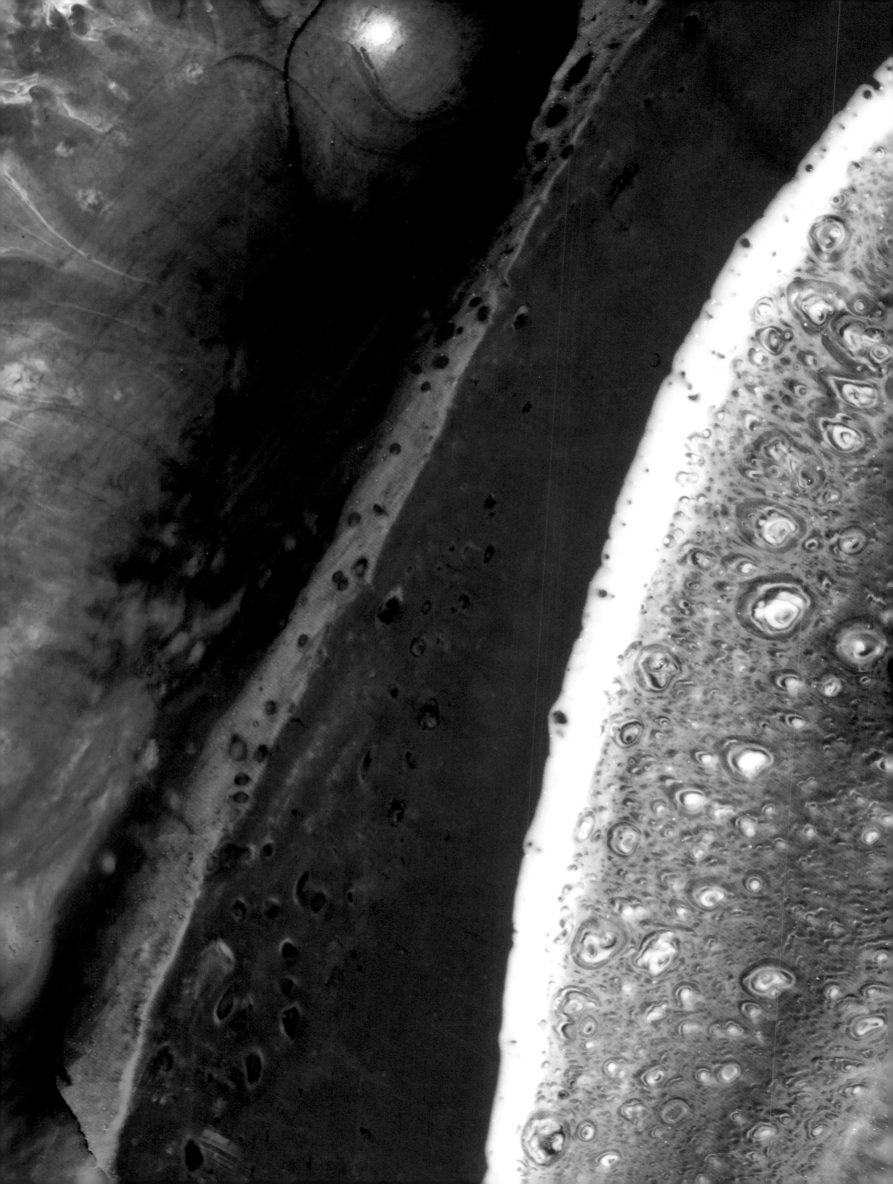

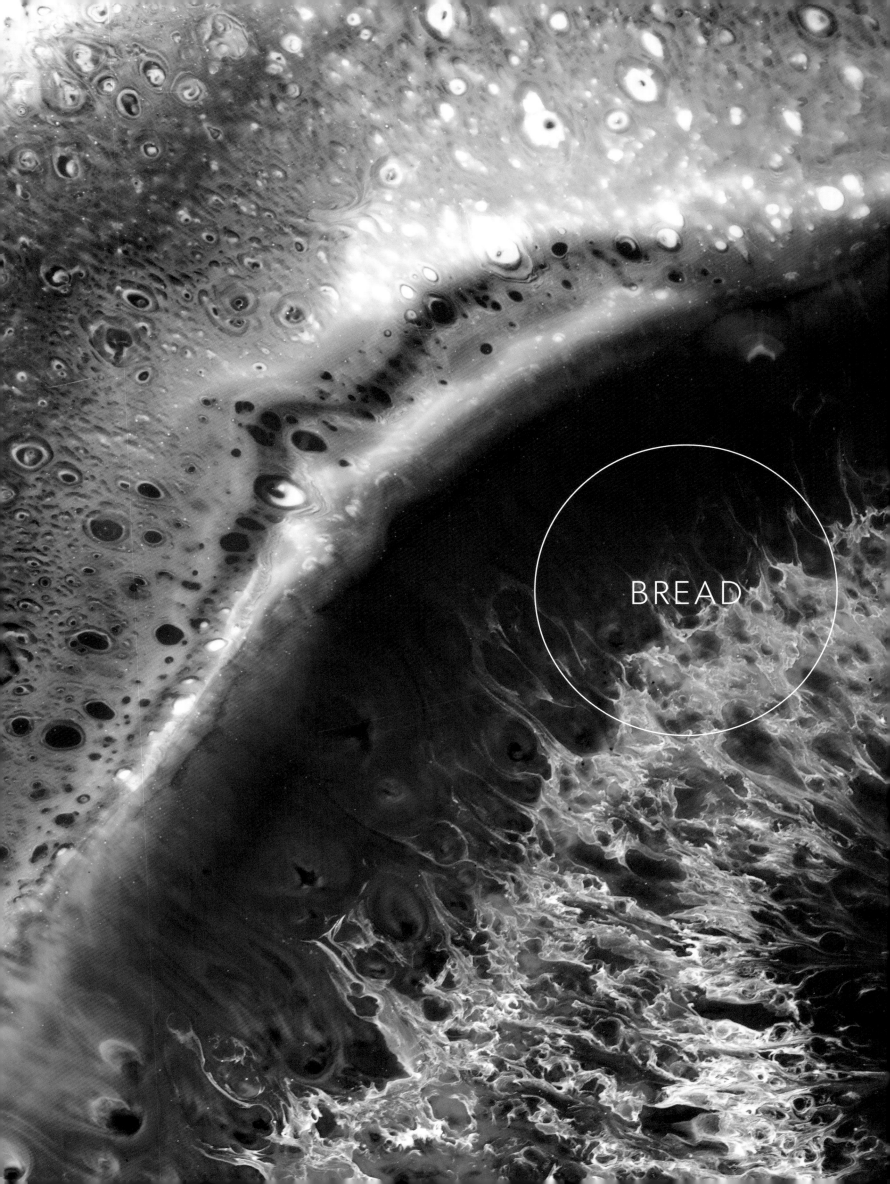

# BREAD

## WHITE FARMHOUSE BREAD

750g T65 white bread flour
425g water
20g fresh yeast
20g fine sea salt

## GRANARY BREAD

750g granary flour
425g water
20g fresh yeast
20g fine sea salt

Both breads are made by the same method.
Mix the flour and the salt.
Dissolve the yeast in tepid water.
Make a well in the flour and add the water.
Knead to a smooth dough.
Prove at an ambient temperature until a third bigger in size.
On a floured table, gently turn the bread and knock back.
Shape, egg wash and flour the loaf.
Score with a razor blade and bake in preheated oven at 220°C until golden underneath.
(This is a very easy recipe to start with and both breads can be flavoured with nuts, seeds and dried fruits. Our favourites include dried fig, smoked apricots, onion seeds, walnuts, wild garlic purée and sunflower seeds).

# RYE AND ONION SEED CRISPBREAD

250g semi skimmed milk
5g fresh yeast
200g rye flour
200g strong white bread flour
20g caster sugar
10g fine sea salt
25g unsalted butter
20g Black onion seeds
Half a teaspoon baking powder
2g ground cumin

Gently heat the milk and butter until lukewarm.
Remove from the heat, whisk in the yeast and dissolve.
Pour onto the other ingredients and mix to a smooth dough, rest for 25 minutes.
Cut in two.
Roll and pass through a pasta machine until the second thinnest setting.
Cut and bake at 180°C for about 9 minutes or until golden.
Remove from the oven and drizzle with a good extra virgin olive oil and rock salt.
Leave to cool then break into desired size pieces.

# OATCAKES

240g oatmeal
240g plain flour
120g soft unsalted butter
1 tablespoon duck fat
1 teaspoon fine sea salt
2 tablespoons cold water

Place all the ingredients into a mixing bowl and set on a low speed with a paddle attachment.
After all the ingredients form a smooth pastry-like dough, rest for an hour then roll out between two sheets of greaseproof paper and freeze for at least 2 hours.
Cut to the desired shape and bake in a preheated oven on 180°C until slightly golden (usually about 14 minutes).
Leave to cool on a wire rack.
Stored in an airtight box these oatcakes will keep for 4 days.

# FOCACCIA

1500g strong bread flour
45g fresh yeast
675g water
40g salt
100g extra virgin olive oil

## FOR THE SALAMOIA

185g water
185g extra virgin olive oil
A little rock salt
Rosemary

Make the first stage of the dough as normal and leave to prove.

Gently turn onto a tray and push to the edges so the dough is about half an inch thick.

Whisk and pour the Salamoia onto the top.

Press in the dimples and garnish with rosemary and a little Maldon sea salt.

Leave to prove for 15 minutes and bake at 200°C until golden and all the Salamoia is soaked up.

# TREACLE AND WHOLEMEAL BREAD

750g T65 strong white bread flour
750g wholemeal flour
600g water
90g fresh yeast
90g soft butter
45g salt
300g black treacle

Preheat the oven to 190°C.

Add the salt to the flour.

Heat the treacle, water and the butter until lukewarm.

Add the yeast and dissolve.

Make a well in the flour and salt and gradually pour in the yeast mixture.

Knead to a smooth dough (you may need to add a little more flour if the dough is a bit too sticky).

Prove in a warm place for an hour (due to the density of this bread it won't double in size when proving).

Turn out onto a floured work surface and knead lightly for a few minutes.

Shape into loaves, egg wash and flour the tops.

Score with a blade and leave to prove for another 35 minutes.

Bake for 35 minutes or until golden on the bottom.

# SMOKED WHOLEMEAL BREAD

900g wholemeal flour
600g T55 oak-smoked white bread flour
35g fresh yeast
40g fine sea salt
75g demerara sugar
850g water

Dissolve the yeast in the water and add to the flour/salt/sugar.

Mix to a smooth dough.

Leave to prove until doubled in size, knock back, shape, egg wash and score.

Prove again and bake at 220°C until golden brown

# POOLISH CIABATTA

### FOR THE HERB-INFUSED OIL

300g extra virgin olive oil
30g thyme
20g rosemary

Warm the oil.
Submerge all the herbs and leave for 2 hours.
Filter off the oil and keep chilled until needed.

### TO MAKE THE STARTER

250g bread flour
180g water
3g yeast

Mix the above ingredients and leave covered at room temperature for 18–24 hours.

### CIABATTA MAIN DOUGH

450g bread flour
14g yeast
360g water
55g herb-infused extra virgin olive oil
17g salt

Mix all of the ingredients and the starter to a smooth dough.
Prove and knock back, shape and prove again.
Heat oven to 230°C.
Bake until golden brown on the bottom.

# POOLISH BAGUETTE

### TO MAKE THE STARTER

6g fresh yeast
350g water
300g bread flour
50g dark rye flour

Mix all the above until a smooth dough and leave at room temp for 18 to 24 hours.

### BAGUETTE

All of the starter
1.3kg bread flour
700g water
24g yeast
38g salt

Mix all the ingredients in an electric mixer with a dough hook on low speed, prove, knock back, shape, egg wash, prove again and bake at 220°C until golden on the bottom.

# BUTTERMILK BREAD

900ml buttermilk
(use the whey left over from making butter)
35g fresh yeast
1500g strong white bread flour
40g fine sea salt

Slightly warm the buttermilk and add the yeast.
Dissolve the yeast in the buttermilk, pour onto the flour and salt, mix and knead to a smooth dough.
Prove until doubled in size.
Knock back and shape.
Egg wash the top, flour and slice with a blade, prove again until 50% bigger.
Bake at 220°C until golden brown.

# BRIOCHE

680g soft butter
50g caster sugar
1000g white flour
145g warm milk
30g fine sea salt
30g fresh yeast
12 eggs

Paste together the butter and the sugar.

In a machine mix the flour, milk, salt and yeast then the eggs and mix to a smooth dough.

Slowly add the butter and beat until smooth and well incorporated.

Wrap in cling film and prove in the fridge until doubled (we prefer to prove our brioche in the fridge, although this takes longer the flavour has more depth).

Gently remove the brioche from its bowl and on a lightly floured surface fold into as many layers without losing too much of the air pockets trapped in the dough.

Divide and put into greased bread tins, prove again and bake.

After 15 minutes brush a little egg wash on the tops and finish baking.

# NAAN BREAD

1kg self-raising flour
2 teaspoons fine sea salt
1 tablespoon caster sugar
Half a teaspoon baking powder
1 egg
200g semi-skimmed milk
400g still mineral water
Vegetable oil
Melted salted butter

Mix all the dry ingredients together.

Whisk the water, milk and egg together and add to the dry ingredients.

Mix to form a slightly sticky dough.

Brush with some vegetable oil and leave to prove for 30 minutes.

Knock the dough back, cut into small pieces and shape into small flat ovals on an oiled tray.

Leave again for 10 mins.

Fry in a hot pan with vegetable oil until golden on both sides.

Drain well and brush with melted butter.

# CULTURED BUTTER

1 litre double cream
500ml buttermilk

In a stainless steel bowl, mix ingredients together and cover with cling film.

Leave to stand at room temperature for 24 hours.

Chill for at least 6 hours.

Place in a food mixer and whisk on medium until the butter and the whey have separated.

Drain off the whey and reserve for later use.

Wash the butter in cold water until the water runs clear.

Drain, season and add your chosen flavour. Some of our favourites are; Marmite, mustard, pink peppercorn, roast shallot/garlic or almost any herb.

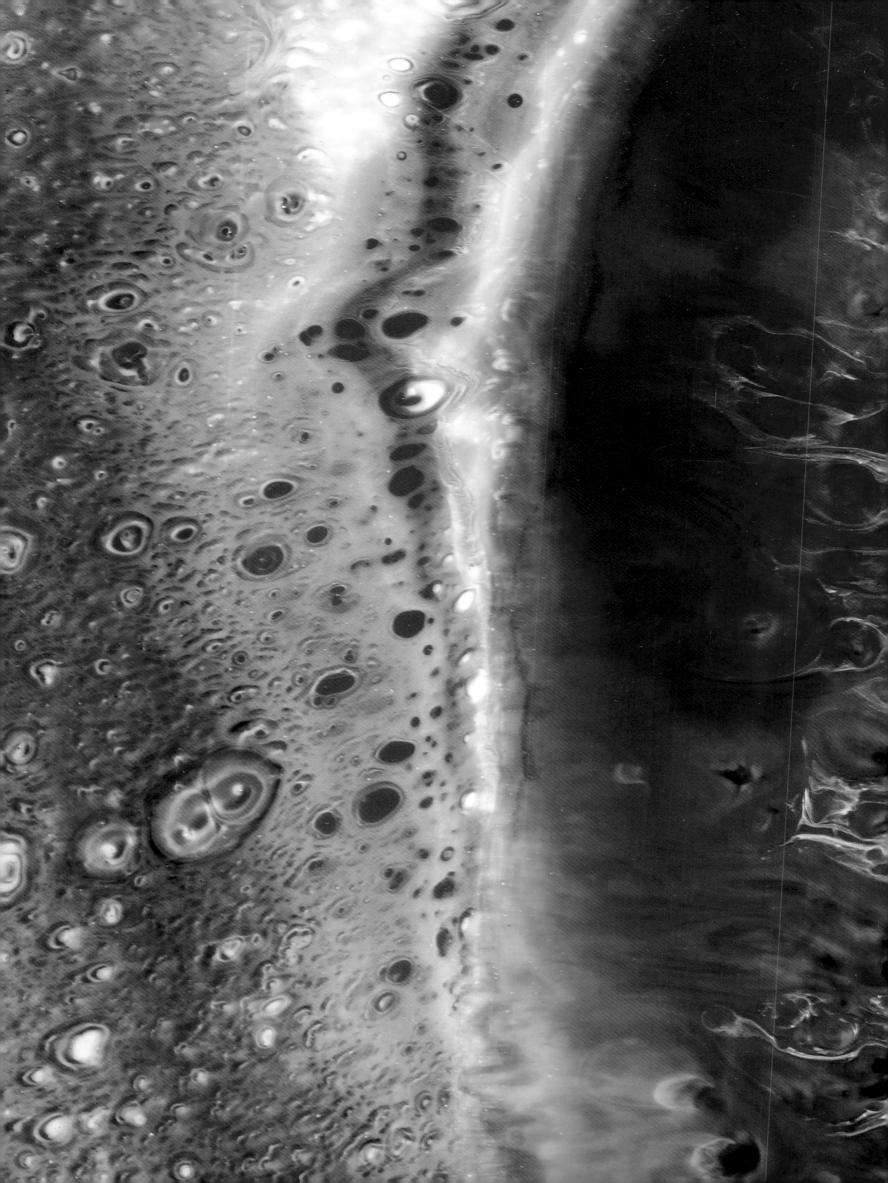

SAVOURY
BUILDING
BLOCKS

# UM BONGO EGG

*"Way down deep in the middle of the Congo, a hippo took an apricot, a guava and a mango. He stuck it with the others and he danced a dainty tango. The rhino said, "I know... we'll call it Um Bongo!" Um Bongo, Um Bongo, they drink it in the Congo! The python picked the passion-fruit, the marmoset the mandarin, the parrot painted packets that the whole caboodle landed in. So when it comes to sun and fun and goodness in the jungle, they all prefer the sunny, funny one they call Um Bongo!"*

## TO SERVE

4 empty egg shells, tops removed with an egg cutter

Sterilise the shell (you can do this by bringing the shell to the boil in some lightly salted water and refreshing it in cold water).

## "YOLK"

200g mango purée
200g apricot purée
50g passion fruit purée
50g guava purée
500g cold water
3.6g Texturas algin
2.6g Texturas citras

In a pan off the heat (it's very important that this is started with cold water), using a small handheld stick blender, blend the citras into the water, followed by the algin.

When both are dissolved, place the pan on the heat and bring to the boil while whisking.

Remove from the heat and leave to cool.

Blend in all the fruit purées, pass through a sieve and chill for at least 5 hours before use.

## CALCIC BATH

500g cold water
3g Texturas calcic

Blend the two together and refrigerate until needed.

## "EGG WHITE"

500g Clementine juice

Distribute the juices evenly (exact amounts are extremely important) between the beakers of a centrifuge and close the lids tightly.

Spin the juice at 6000 rpm for 35 minutes until the juices have separated.

Gently pour off the transparent juice through a J-cloth, leaving the orange solid in the bottom.

Chill the juice until needed and discard the small amount of orange solids.

## MAKING THE UM BONGO EGG

Remove the yolk mix and the calcic bath from the fridge.

Using a small hemispherical spoon, carefully drop in small yolk-sized portions of the Um Bongo yolk into the bath.

Leave for 2 minutes.

Remove with a slotted spoon and transfer to a container of cold water (these can be kept in a fridge in the water for up to 5 hours).

Pour 15g of the transparent clementine juice into a sterilised empty eggshell and carefully place a "yolk" into it.

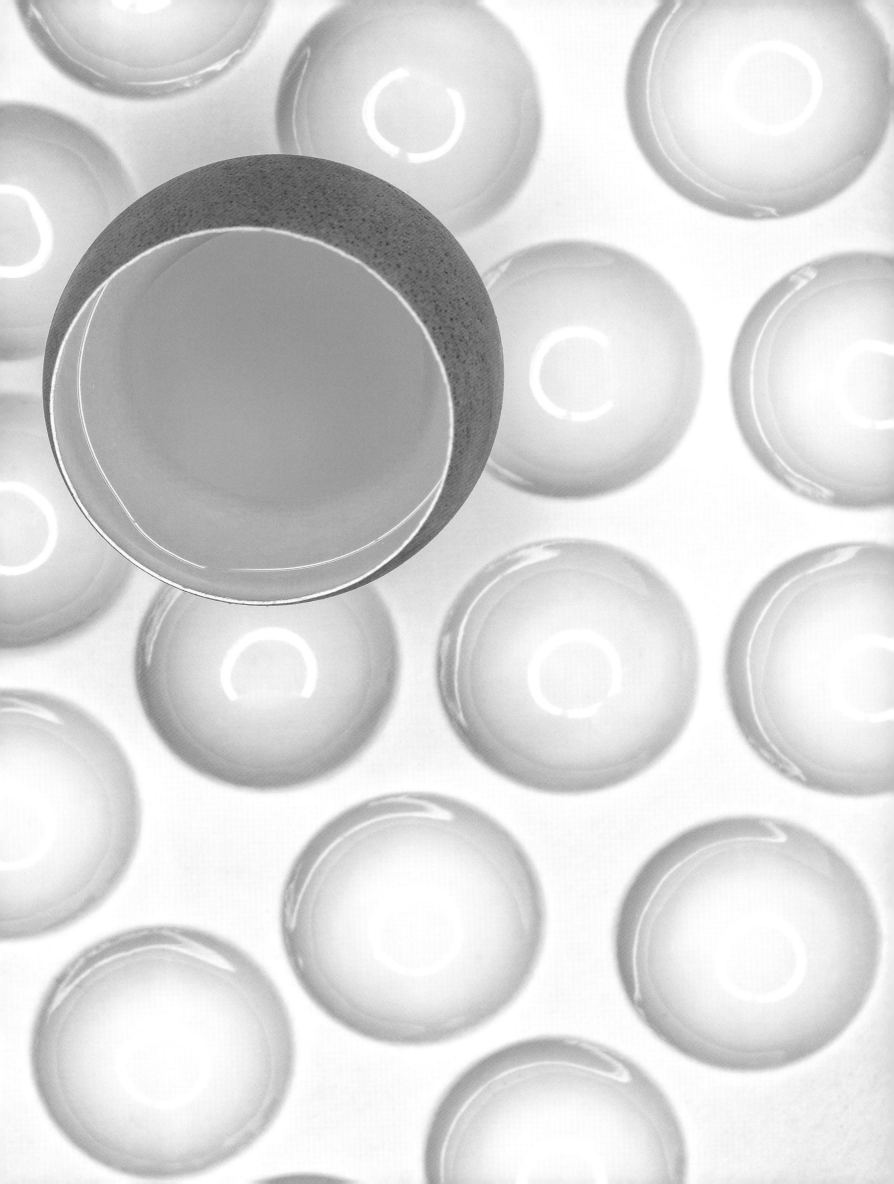

# RADISH POT

### RADISH

4 young breakfast radishes with the leaves intact

### "SOIL"

Extra virgin olive oil
300g button mushrooms
300g good quality black pitted olives
250g ground almonds
40g Texturas Malto

Finely slice the mushrooms and pitted olives. Mix together.

In a medium frying pan and in small batches, sauté the mushroom and olive mix in olive oil until soft (about 4 minutes).

Drain in a colander.

When well drained, spread on a lined try and dehydrate at 45°C for 12 hours.

In small batches, blend in a food processor with the almonds and malto until a dark soil-like texture (if a little too moist and not crumbly enough, add a little more ground almond).

### SMOKED MACKEREL MOUSSE

2 smoked peppered mackerel fillets, skin and bones removed
300g cream cheese
Juice of one lemon
Seasoning

In a food processor, blend the mackerel fillets for 1 minute, add the cream cheese and blend for a further 2 minutes. Add the lemon juice and check for seasoning.

Transfer to a box with a tight-fitting lid and store in the fridge.

### TO SERVE

Small ceramic plant pots

# OLD CHEWY CARROTS

8 medium carrots
120g caster sugar
50g butter
15 coffee beans
Pinch of fine sea salt
50g Texturas Malto

Set your water bath to 90°C.

Peel, top and tail the carrots.

Put the carrots and caster sugar in a vac pac bag and seal on maximum.

Place in the water bath and cook until tender (about 70 minutes).

Open the bag and refresh in iced water.

Place the carrots on a lined dehydrator tray and dry at 52°C until half the size (about 6 hours).

(When dried, the carrots can be kept in a sealed box in the fridge for up to 3 days).

Meanwhile, warm the butter in a small saucepan, add the coffee beans and season with the salt.

Remove from the heat and leave to infuse for 10 minutes.

Pass through a fine sieve.

Put half of the infused butter into a bowl and, using a whisk, incorporate the Malto until you have a lump-free coffee butter powder. (This can be stored at room temperature for up to a week).

Heat the remaining infused butter in a pan, add the carrots and slightly caramelise all over.

Finish with the coffee butter powder.

# SMOKED PARMESAN AGNOLOTTI

## PASTA DOUGH

300g pasta flour
15g fine sea salt
160g egg yolks
1 whole egg
1 tbsp oil

Mix the salt and the flour together in a bowl.

Make a well in the centre of the flour and add the yolks, eggs and oil.

Work all the ingredients to a smooth dough and knead for 10 minutes.

Rest for at least an hour (depending on the humidity of the flour, pasta will sometimes need a little more egg yolk or flour).

The dough should be soft and supple.

## FILLING

830g water
5 sprigs of thyme
10g bonfire salt
(heavily smoked, dark sea salt, available online)
65g smoked butter
30g black truffle oil
20g extra virgin olive oil
115g smoked polenta
145g finely-grated Parmesan

Bring the water, thyme and bonfire salt to the boil.

Remove from the heat and leave to infuse for 20 minutes.

Remove the thyme and bring the water back up to the boil.

Sprinkle in the polenta and whisk.

Turn the heat down low and cook for 25 minutes.

Remove from the heat and cool slightly.

Transfer to a food blender and turn on medium.

Add all the other ingredients and blend until smooth.

Check seasoning.

Chill until set.

## TO MAKE THE AGNOLOTTI

Transfer the filling to a piping bag.

Using a pasta machine, roll out the pasta starting on the thickest setting.

Roll through the different settings twice on each one right to the thinnest.

Pipe a line of the filling 3cm in from the edge along the length of the sheet of pasta and roll the pasta over, encasing the filling.

Pinch the filling at 3cm gaps.

Using a pasta wheel cutter, cut the strip of agnolotti lengthways and then cut through pinch marks.

Store on a little polenta in the fridge until needed.

Cook in simmering salted water for 1 minute (due to delicate nature of filled fresh egg pasta, boiling water is a little too harsh).

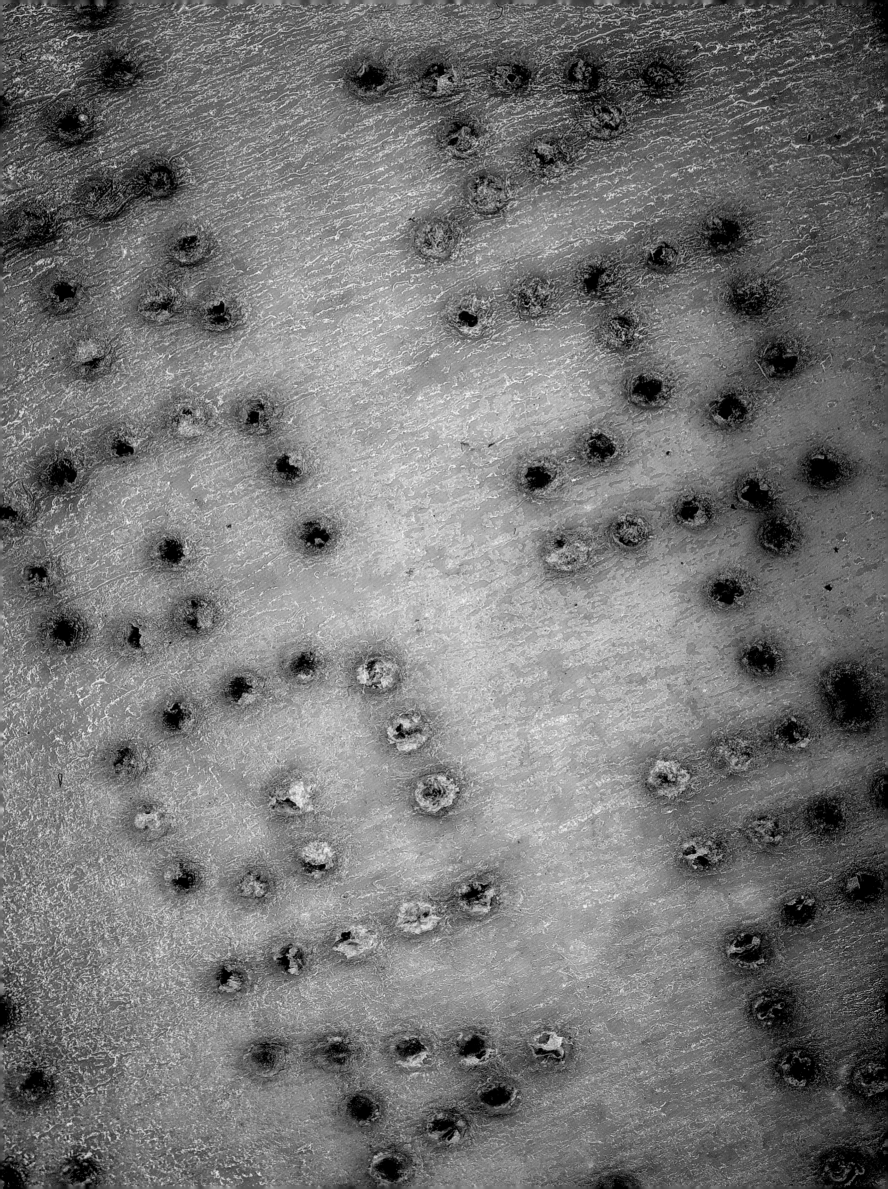

# LOBSTER CORAL CAVATELLI

*Raw lobster coral can be kept frozen until you have enough for this recipe.*

*The raw dough is a deep green colour but as soon as it hits the boiling salted water it turns to a vibrant red.*

## PASTA DOUGH

300g flour

15g fine sea salt

90g yolks

70g raw lobster coral

1 whole egg

10g extra virgin olive oil, plus a little extra to coat the blanched cavatelli

1 pasta machine with a gnocchi/cavatelli attachment (available online)

1 pan of boiling salted water

1 stainless steel bowl with iced water

Mix the salt and the flour together.

In a food processor blend the lobster coral and eggs until smooth.

Make a well in the centre of the flour and add the yolks, egg, lobster coral mix and oil.

Work all the ingredients to a smooth dough and knead for 10 minutes.

Rest for at least an hour.

Adjust the consistency of the dough with a little more egg yolk or flour, it should be soft and supple.

Cut into six pieces and roll into 1cm thick cigar-shaped ropes.

Flour lightly and pass through a cavatelli attachment on your pasta machine.

Blanch in boiling salted water for 30 seconds and refresh in the iced water.

When cold, drain well and coat in a little extra virgin olive.

Stored in an airtight box in the fridge, the cavatelli will keep for 3 days.

# CLASSIC GNOCCHI

900g mash made from scooped-out baked potatoes
2 eggs
325g plain flour
150g grated Parmesan
Seasoning

Pass the mash through a fine sieve.

Beat in the eggs and seasoning.

Add the flour when the potato mix is completely cold and mix to a smooth dough.

Roll small cigar shapes and cut with a floured knife.

Blanch in boiling salted water until the dumplings float, then plunge into iced water.

Drain and toss in a little extra virgin olive oil.

The gnocchi are now ready to use (they can be stored in the fridge for up to 3 days).

# TOAST GNOCCHI

460g day-old bread (focaccia or ciabatta are best)
300g semi skimmed milk
2 eggs
5g fresh sage, finely chopped
5g fresh rosemary, finely chopped
10g fine sea salt
220g plain flour (maybe a little more)
5g cracked black pepper
Fresh sage, to finish

Slice the stale bread and toast under a hot grill.

Blend the toast to a fine breadcrumb and add the milk.

Leave for 40 minutes.

Squeeze out any excess milk (there won't be much, if any at all).

Mix in the eggs.

Add the chopped sage and rosemary, salt, flour and pepper.

Mix to a smooth dough.

On a floured work surface, cut the dough into five pieces and roll each into a long 1cm-thick cigar shape.

Cut the gnocchi to the desired shape and size (usually around 1cm long on a slight angle).

Blanch in boiling salted water until they float (usually around 45 seconds).

Refresh in iced water.

Drain and coat in a little extra virgin olive oil.

These can now be kept in the fridge for up to 3 days.

To serve, sauté in a little olive oil and lightly season.

When nicely coloured, add a small amount of butter and fresh sage and check the seasoning.

# CORNED BEEF

1750 ml cold water

90g fine sea salt

3kg brisket

30g gelatine leaves, soaked

Make a brine with the water and salt and place the beef in the liquid.

Refrigerate for 3 days.

Thoroughly wash the beef, place in a pan of cold water and gradually bring up to a simmer.

Slowly cook until the meat is very tender (you may have to top up the water).

Take off the heat and carefully remove the meat from the stock.

Pick off any excess lumps of fat (don't remove all the fat as this will make the corned beef dry).

Flake the brisket into a clean bowl.

Return the stock to the heat and reduce until syrupy.

Add the gelatine and stir until dissolved.

Pass the reduced stock through a sieve onto the flaked brisket.

Check the seasoning.

Press into a terrine mould or loaf tin lined with cling film.

Press with a heavy weight on top and chill until set.

# SMOKED HADDOCK GOUGERES

200g semi-skimmed milk

200g water

100g unsalted butter

250g plain flour

6 medium eggs

170g grated Gruyere

170g grated Parmesan

Maldon sea salt

Boil the milk, water, butter and a pinch of salt.

Add the flour, stirring so all the flour is incorporated, and cook on the side of the stove until the mix comes away from the side of the pan.

Remove from the heat.

Place in a mixer with a paddle on a slow speed for a couple of minutes to cool slightly, then add the eggs one at a time, then the cheese.

Pipe on a lined tray and bake at 180°C for 15–20 minutes or until golden.

## SMOKED HADDOCK FILLING

200g undyed smoked haddock, skinned and boned

100g water

150g double cream

A few thyme leaves

Place all the ingredients in a small saucepan and cook over a low heat until the smoked haddock starts to flake.

Remove from the heat and cool a little.

With an electric hand blender, blend the filling until smooth.

Transfer to a piping bag and chill.

Make a small hole at the bottom of the gougeres and fill with the smoked haddock filling.

Serve at room temperature.

# VEGETABLES À LA GRECQUE WITH MORTEAU SAUSAGE

125g extra virgin olive oil

250g white wine

500g water

125g white wine vinegar

3 bay leaves

10 green peppercorns

A few small sprigs of rosemary and thyme

Sea salt

1 teaspoon fennel seeds

Small dice of carrots, celery, shallot rings, fennel, chestnut mushrooms and Morteau sausage

Bring all the liquid ingredients to a boil.

Add the peppercorns, herbs, fennel seeds and seasoning.

Half cook the vegetables, one type at a time and leave to cool on a tray.

Lastly, add the Morteau sausage and reduce the stock by half.

Remove from the heat and leave to cool.

When cold, add all the other vegetables and store chilled in an airtight box until needed.

# LACE TUILE

20g strong flour

600g water

Whisk the two ingredients together, making sure there are no lumps.

Place a 7 inch non-stick pan over a high heat and using a 50g ladle, pour into the hot pan.

The mixture will reduce as it starts to become a light golden colour.

Turn the heat down for the last 30 seconds and then remove from the heat.

With a palette knife, remove the lace tuile from the pan and store on absorbent paper in an airtight box until needed.

# SQUID INK LACE TUILE

5g squid ink

80g water

20g vegetable oil

Whisk all the ingredients together and repeat the same method as the Lace Tuile (bearing in mind this won't go golden as it's a black tuile).

# BURNT CITRUS JELLY

140g caster sugar

A couple of zests from an orange, grapefruit and lemon, lightly blowtorched

520g of juice consisting of equal quantities of lemon, grapefruit and orange

8 leaves of gelatine soaked and squeezed

Caramelise the sugar.

Add the juice and zest, then the gelatine, whisk until dissolved.

Pass through a sieve.

Chill to set.

Cut with a warm knife.

# FIZZY GRAPES

150g white or red seedless grapes, cut in half
1 litre syphon gun with two CO² chargers

Place the grapes inside the soda syphon gun, screw on the lid and discharge the two CO² chargers.

Agitate slightly but don't shake too hard as it will damage the grapes.

Chill for at least 4 hours.

When needed, place a cloth over the nozzle and gently release the gas.

*Very important: release the gas before you unscrew the top.*

This method of carbonation can be done with any fruits high in juice content such as melon, grapes, pineapple, orange or grapefruit.

# PERNOD GRAPES

4 star anise
300g water
80g lemon juice
20g Pernod
60g caster sugar
1 bunch seedless red or white grapes
A few sprigs of thyme

Mix all the ingredients except the grapes together.

Pour into a vac pac bag with the grapes.

Seal and cook in a water bath set on 55°C for an hour, then chill in an ice bath.

Refrigerate in bags until needed.

# EDIBLE MUSSEL SHELLS

200g pasta flour
100g water
20g squid ink
5g fine sea salt
40 mussel shell halves, emptied, cleaned and completely dried

Make a smooth black dough from the first four ingredients, cover with cling film and leave to rest in the fridge for at least 4 hours.

Oil the mussel shells liberally.

Roll the dough through a pasta machine, and line two mussel shells that are tight fitting together.

Press together making sure the dough overlaps the lip of the shell.

Fry at 180°C for a few minutes.

*(The shells will need a little pressure to hold them together for the first minute or so of cooking; we use the tips of plating tweezers, but be extremely careful not to burn yourself).*

# CURED EGG YOLK

700g  fine sea salt
200g caster sugar
12 egg yolks
A little olive oil

Combine the fine sea salt and caster sugar and pour three quarters of the mixture into a flat stainless steel tray.

With the back of a spoon, make 12 dimples in the mixture.

Separate the eggs and carefully lay each yolk in a dimple.

Cover the tops of the yolks with the rest of the sugar and salt mixture.

Cover with cling film and leave in the fridge.

After 2 days, turn the yolks over with a spoon.

Leave to rest for another day.

Remove from the fridge, discard the tray and wash the firm yolks in iced water.

Brush a dehydrator tray with a little olive oil (this will prevent the yolks sticking when drying). Dry on 63°C for 10 hours.

Refrigerate until needed.

These yolks will keep chilled for 2 weeks.

Grated on a fine microplane, these cured yolks add an amazing texture to fish, shellfish and fresh pasta.

# PEA MOUSSE

2½ gelatine leaves, soaked in cold water
200ml double cream
A few drops of lemon juice
600g frozen petit pois
Salt and sugar to taste

Lightly whip the cream.

Blanch the peas in boiling salted water.

Drain, reserving some of the water.

In a food processor blend the peas with the salt, sugar and the soaked gelatine, adding some of the cooking water as needed.

Blend until smooth.

Pass through a sieve and leave to cool slightly.

Fold in the cream.

Check for seasoning and chill until set.

# SEMI-DRIED CHERRY TOMATOES

500g cherry tomatoes
200g caster sugar
5 shreds lemon peel
350g herb-infused oil

Score the cherry tomatoes and blanch for 10 seconds.

Refresh in iced water and peel.

Roll the peeled cherry tomatoes in the caster sugar, place on a lined tray and dehydrate on 40°C for 4-5 hours or until 30% smaller.

Leave to cool.

Place the lemon peel and tomatoes in the herb oil and store chilled in an airtight box until needed.

# CAPER CRUMBLE

100g capers
120g unsalted butter, soft
20g egg yolk
10g white wine caper vinegar (from the caper jar)
60g ground almonds
150g plain flour
4g fresh yeast

Preheat oven to 175°C.
In a food processor, blend the capers and the butter.
Add all the other ingredients.
Bake on a lined tray at 175°C until a light golden colour (about 7 minutes).
Leave to cool.
Blend to a fine sand-like texture and store in an airtight box.

# PINEAPPLE AND MUSTARD PICKLE

2 medium pineapples
2 cloves
1 dessert spoon good quality grain mustard
6 tablespoons white wine vinegar
300g demerara sugar

Peel, core and dice the pineapples into 1cm cubes.
Place all the ingredients into a suitably sized saucepan and bring to the boil.
Turn the heat down and cook until slightly caramelised.
Remove from heat and leave to cool.
Discard the cloves and store in an airtight container in the fridge.

# CHORIZO AND APPLE JAM

200g sweet artisan chorizo finely diced
1kg cooking apples peeled and diced
1 litre of water
Sugar and seasoning to taste
A few branches of thyme tied together

Place the chorizo, thyme and water in a pan and reduce until three quarters of the water has evaporated.
Add the apples and reduce on a lower heat until all the water has been absorbed.
Season with sugar and salt to taste and remove the thyme.
Chill.

# CHORIZO, PEACH AND ROSEMARY COMPOTE

4 shallots, finely diced
20g soft dark brown sugar
140g white balsamic or white wine vinegar
150g chorizo, finely diced
8 ripe peaches, finely diced
4g fresh rosemary leaves, finely chopped
Olive oil
Seasoning

Sweat the shallots in a little olive oil, add the sugar and caramelise slightly, season.
Add the vinegar, reduce by half and add the chorizo and peaches.
Gently mix, turn the heat to low, cover with greaseproof paper and simmer until soft (about 40 minutes).
Check for seasoning and sharpness, adjusting with a little vinegar if needed.
Add the rosemary, mix and remove from the heat.
Chill.

# BLOOD ORANGE JAM

1kg blood orange juice
1kg caster sugar
3kg blood oranges
500g extra virgin olive oil
2 dessert spoons xanthan gum

Boil the juice and sugar and leave to cool.
Strain.
Pierce the oranges and boil them in water.
Change the water and repeat this three times.
Cut into quarters, remove all pips and cook further in the juice.
Blend in the Thermomix and add the olive oil.
Slowly add the xanthan until the right consistency is obtained.

# GRANNY SMITH, PEAR AND VANILLA CHUTNEY

500g Granny Smiths apples
500g pears
3 banana shallots, finely diced
200g cider vinegar or white wine vinegar
1 split and scraped vanilla pod
A small pinch of fine sea salt
400g caster sugar

Core and large dice the apples and pears.
Place everything in a large saucepan and using a high heat, bring to the boil.
Turn the heat down to a simmer and reduce until slightly caramelised.

# CHARENTAIS MELON MUSTARD FRUIT

800g orange fleshed melon, diced
2 teaspoons good quality grain mustard
80g water
500g caster sugar
375g white wine vinegar
1 cinnamon stick
1½ tablespoons fine sea salt
1kg ice

Sprinkle the melon with the salt and ice.
Leave for 30 minutes then wash well and dry.
Mix together the vinegar and sugar, add the fruit and leave for a few hours
Add the water and cinnamon stick, bring to the boil and reduce until syrupy.
Mix in the mustard and chill.

# BEER-PICKLED ONIONS

5 bunches of grelot onions (just the bulb part)
400g ale
180g honey
220g white balsamic or white wine vinegar
1 teaspoon fine sea salt
A few sprigs of rosemary and thyme

Cut the bulb onions in half and blanch in boiling salted water for 20 seconds.
Separate all the layers so the onions are in petal-shaped cups.
Boil the ale, honey, herbs and vinegar.
Leave to cool slightly and pour onto the onion cups.
When cold, store in a sterilised jar or vac pac and leave for at least 24 hours before using.

# PICKLED ROSE PETALS

440g water
250g beetroot juice
50g rose water
105g caster sugar
70g white wine or white balsamic vinegar
2g malic acid
2g salt
35g lemon juice

Boil all the ingredients and leave to cool.

4 red roses

Remove the petals from the roses, discarding any damaged ones.
Blanche the petals in boiling water for 1 minute and refresh in iced water.
Drain and add to the cooled pickling liquor.
Leave for at least 24 hours before use.
Store in the refrigerator.

# PICKLED PEPPERS

600g white wine vinegar
70g caster sugar
22g salt
300g water
4 cloves
3 bay leaves
6 bell peppers

Preheat oven to 200°C.
Roast the peppers in the oven for 15 minutes.
Place all the other ingredients in a pan, bring to the boil and reduce by half.
Pass through a sieve and leave to cool.
Remove the peppers from the oven and blowtorch the skins until black and blistered.
While warm, place in a bowl and cover with cling film (this will help steam the skins off).
When cool, scrape the skins and seeds off the peppers.
Rinse the peppers clean.
Cut to the desired shape and size.
Seal the peppers with the cool pickling liquor in a vac pac bag and leave for at least 24 hours before using.

# PICKLED PINE SHOOTS

*In early spring, light green tender shoots appear on the ends of the pine branches. These make good eating.*

30 small sprigs of young light green pine shoots
100g white balsamic vinegar
100g water
Small pinch of fine sea salt

Place the shoots in a vac pac bag, add all the other ingredients and seal on 100% vacuum.
Leave for at least 24 hours before using.

# SOUS VIDE GOOSEBERRIES

300g green gooseberries
2 sprigs of thyme
320g caster sugar
180g water

Bring the water, sugar and thyme to the boil. Remove from the heat and chill.
When cold place in a vac pac bag along with the gooseberries.
Seal and poach in a water bath set at 45°C for 3 hours.

# CONFIT PINEAPPLE

2 pineapples, peeled, quartered and cored
Spices for each quarter piece of pineapple
(makes one spice bag)
2 cloves
1 cardamom pod, crushed
2g allspice
1 star anise

Vacuum pack the pineapple quarters individually with the spices and cook in a water bath at 58°C for 3 hours.
Cool in an ice bath.
Leave sealed with the spices and refrigerate until needed.

# SPHERICAL POTATOES

750g potatoes, peeled and cut in identically-sized pieces
1.5 litres water
Chopped herbs (rosemary, thyme, parsley)
Seasoning
Algin thickener
70g extra virgin olive oil
(other nut or flavoured oils will work as well )
In a calcic bath; 1 litre cold water, 10g calcic

Gently cook the potatoes until tender, then drain.
Reserve 1020g of the potato water and blend in a Thermomix with the potatoes, oil and algin.
Check seasoning.
Pass through a sieve then transfer to a piping bag and chill.
When cool, fill hemispherical moulds and freeze.
Once frozen, these can be kept in a sealed box for up to 10 days.
When needed, drop the frozen potato into the calcic bath and leave for 2 minutes.
Remove with a slotted spoon and leave to defrost in cold water.

# POTATO PURÉE

1kg unwashed Maris Piper potatoes
400g double cream
100g water
Fine sea salt
Latex gloves
Drum sieve

Preheat the oven to 200°C.
Wash the potatoes thoroughly and, while wet, roll in fine sea salt.
Place on a tray and bake in the oven until the centre is soft when checked with a sharp knife.

Leave to cool for 5 minutes.
Wearing latex gloves, cut the potatoes in half and use a spoon to scoop out the flesh.
Pass through the drum sieve (the potato must be hot otherwise it won't go through).
Place the purée into a stainless steel bowl.
Boil the cream, water and a good pinch of salt.
Add the boiling cream onto the purée and whisk to incorporate, slowly at first, to achieve the desired consistency.
Season.

# WARM POTATO ESPUMA

600g maris piper potatoes, unwashed
300g milk
50g unsalted smoked butter
Smoked salt

Set a water bath to 58°C.

Peel the potatoes and cut into 2cm dice.

Cook in lightly salted water.

Drain when cooked, reserving 120g of the cooking liquor.

Transfer the potatoes to a blender, add the milk and the reserved cooking water.

Blend until smooth.

Add the butter and blend until completely incorporated.

Check the seasoning and pass through a fine sieve.

Pour into a 1 litre syphon gun and charge with 2 N²O cartridges.

Shake well for 30 seconds and keep warm in the water bath at 58°C until needed.

# BROWN SAUCE

1 onion, finely chopped
5 cloves
1 star anise
80g dried dates
65g soft dark brown sugar
70g black treacle
2 dessert spoons concentrated tamarind paste
325g tomatoes,chopped
450g malt vinegar
1 dessert spoon grain mustard
1 tsp ground ginger
1 dessert spoon ground allspice
Seasoning
Xanthan gum (optional)

Sweat the onions in a little oil, add all the other ingredients and slowly cook for 40 minutes. Allow to cool.

When just warm, transfer to a blender and purée until smooth.

Add a small amount of xanthan gum powder if needed, to thicken the sauce slightly.

Pass through a sieve and store in the fridge in a container with a tight fitting lid or an airtight sauce bottle.

# BLACK GARLIC SAUCE

150g gem lettuce
10g unsalted butter, melted
65g black garlic
140g chicken/vegetable stock
Small pinch xanthan gum
15g toasted sesame oil
Maldon salt

Griddle the lettuce in a pan, season and baste with butter until dark brown.

Add all the other ingredients except the xanthan and simmer for 10 minutes.

Transfer to a blender and blend until smooth.

Add the xanthan.

Pass through a sieve and check for seasoning.

# XO SAUCE

200g smoked Morteau sausage

7 shallots

125g fresh ginger

Large pinch of sugar

4 garlic cloves

3 red chillies (medium heat)

100g mirin

12g bonito flakes

200g light soy sauce

25g roast prawn powder (as used in the prawn satay recipe)

1 litre vegetable oil

300g toasted sesame oil

Dice the smoked sausage.

Peel the shallots and dice with the garlic and chillies.

In a little of the vegetable oil sauté the shallots, garlic and chilli for 2 minutes until nicely coloured.

Add the sugar and caramelise.

Deglaze the pan with the mirin, then add the diced smoked sausage and other ingredients.

Turn down the heat and cook slowly for one hour.

Transfer to a food processor and blend until smooth.

Check the seasoning and pass through a fine sieve.

# PONZU SAUCE

100g light soy sauce

100g dark soy sauce

35g fresh yuzu juice

250g rice wine vinegar

200g mirin

100g fresh ginger, finely chopped

100g sunflower oil

20g fresh coriander

1 teaspoon xanthan gum

In a food processor, blend all the ingredients until smooth and well-incorporated.

Thicken with a little xanthan gum and pass through a sieve.

When serving, bring the sauce up to a simmer (not a boil as it will split).

137

# CHICKEN FAT MAYONNAISE

100g egg yolks

15g white wine vinegar or white balsamic

15g Dijon mustard

Large pinch of Maldon salt

15g cold water

200g warm melted roast chicken fat

30g thyme, chives and chervil, finely chopped

Blend the egg yolks, mustard and vinegar together in a blender, and season.

Slowly add the warm chicken fat, then the cold water and lastly the herbs.

Check for seasoning and if not quite sharp enough add a few more drops of vinegar.

Chill until ready to use.

# GOLDEN RAISIN DRESSING

100g golden raisins
100g capers
120g water
Seasoning if needed

Blend all the ingredients in a food blender on high speed until smooth.
Pass through a sieve.
Store in a plastic bottle in the fridge until needed

# HAZELNUT, THYME AND PARMESAN PESTO

150g roasted hazelnuts with the husks removed
50g grated Parmesan
10g fresh thyme leaves
100g hazelnut oil
Seasoning, to taste

Blend all the ingredients in a food processor to a smooth paste.

# SOFT EGG AND OLIVE OIL EMULSION

3 medium free range eggs
3 small shallots, finely diced
300ml extra virgin olive oil
75ml white wine vinegar
Seasoning

Sweat the shallots in a small amount of olive oil until translucent.
Remove from the heat and leave to cool.
Place the eggs into boiling water and cook for 4 ½ minutes.
Refresh in iced water and peel.
In a food processor, add the cold soft-cooked eggs and the shallots.
Add the vinegar and blend until smooth.
Slowly add the olive oil in a steady trickle as if making mayonnaise.
Season and store in the fridge until needed.

# CHARCOAL

250g Maldon sea salt
1 small lump of charcoal (about 20g)
1 lemon, zested

Microplane the charcoal.
Mix all the ingredients together and keep in a sealed jar.

# COAL OIL

500ml olive oil
6 pieces charcoal

Get the charcoal burning by placing it over a gas hob.
Once it is lit, let it burn until it turns white and the flames go out.
Being careful not to burn yourself, take a pair of tongs and place the hot coals into the olive oil.
Leave to cool down, allowing the charcoal sediment to settle on the bottom of the pan.
Leave for at least 3 hours then gently take the oil from the top leaving any debris at the bottom.

# CITRUS OIL

100g citrus peel, from either pink grapefruit, lemon, lime, bergamot or orange
350g olive oil

Warm the olive oil to 60°C and pour onto the citrus peels.
Store in the fridge in an airtight box for 2 days.
Remove from the fridge and let the oil come to room temperature.
Pour through a fine sieve and discard the peels.
Reserve.

# BEECH LEAF OIL

150g young beech leaves
100g flat leaf parsley
500g pommice oil

Blend everything in a Thermomix for 7 minutes, strain through a J-cloth.
Vac pac until needed.

# POWDERS

*Most of the powders we use will follow the same method and principles as in this red cabbage powder. At the restaurant there are several that we use to bring a different taste or texture to a dish in a way not expected.*

*These powders will keep for up to 1 month if kept in a dry cool place.*

## RED CABBAGE POWDER

**1 medium sized red cabbage, broken up into leaves**

Bring a large pot of salted water to the boil.

Blanch the red cabbage for 1 minute then refresh in iced water and drain.

Transfer to a dehydrator set at 45°C until dry.

Blend in a food processor or spice grinder.

Pass through a sieve and store at room temperature in an airtight box.

Here are a few ideas for other vegetable powders that work with the same method;

kale, cavolo nero, Savoy cabbage, peas, broad beans.

## SQUID INK AND VINEGAR POWDER

**5 slices of medium cut white bread**
**5 x 2g sachets squid ink**
**(available from fishmongers or online)**
**200g white wine vinegar**
**Water as needed**
**Fine sea salt**
**Xanthan gum, as needed**

Place all the ingredients except the xanthan in a food processor and blend until smooth (the amount of water you need will depend on the bread), add enough water to make it blend easily in the processor.

Thicken with the xanthan gum and season.

Spread onto a lined dehydrator tray and dry at 52°C until breakable (about 12 hours).

Blend in a spice grinder and pass through a fine sieve.

Store in a cool place in an airtight box.

# ROOT VEGETABLE POWDERS

*This method will also work with root vegetables such as turnip, carrot, swede and parsnip.*

## PARSNIP POWDER

**500g parsnips, cut into large pieces**
**Xanthan gum (as needed)**

Bring a large pan of salted water up to the boil.

Add the parsnips and cook until soft.

Remove from the water and transfer to a blender, using a little of the cooking water to help blend the parsnips until smooth.

Add a little xanthan gum to make the purée slightly thicker.

Season.

Spread on a lined dehydrator tray and set on 45°C until dry (this usually takes around 10 hours).

Break up the purée and blend either in a food processor or spice grinder.

Pass through a sieve.

Store in an airtight container.

## ROAST ONION POWDER

**1kg onions**
**Extra virgin olive oil**
**Water, as needed**
**2 large sprigs thyme**
**Seasoning**
**10g xanthan gum**

Peel and slice the onions.

In a saucepan sweat the onions over a high heat with the thyme in the olive oil.

When the onions start to caramelise, turn down the heat and continue to cook until a very dark brown.

Transfer to a blender and purée with the water, adding just enough for the onions to blend with ease.

Thicken with the xanthan and check for seasoning.

Spread onto a lined dehydrator tray and dry at 45°C until breakable.

Blend in a spice grinder, pass through a sieve and store in an airtight box. Remember that with seasoning powders, the salt content will get stronger as they dry.

# JUS GRAS

2kg chicken wings

2 onions

2 carrots

1 medium leek

10 black peppercorns

2 bay leaves

250g light bodied red wine

1 teaspoon tomato purée

Olive oil

1.2g xanthan gum

25g soy lecithin powder

120g roast chicken fat (ask your butcher for excess chicken skin, they will have plenty)

Fine sea salt, to taste

A few drops of fresh lemon juice

Preheat oven to 200°C.

Roast the skin in the oven with a bay leaf, a few peppercorns and a sprinkle of sea salt.

When the skin is golden remove from the oven and leave to cool for a few minutes.

Pass the fat through a fine sieve, reserving the skin.

Roast the chicken wings until dark and golden, remove from the oven and leave to cool slightly.

Finely dice the leek, onion and carrot.

In a medium saucepan, add the olive oil and fry off the onion, leek and carrot until golden.

Add the bay leaf, peppercorns and tomato purée.

Fry for a further minute and pour in the red wine.

Place the chicken wings and the reserved roast chicken skin into the saucepan.

Add enough cold water just to cover and bring to the boil.

Turn down to a simmer and cook for 2½ hours.

Remove from the heat and leave to rest for 20 minutes.

Pass the stock through a sieve.

Return the stock to a high heat and reduce by half (or until a thicker consistency and a good flavour).

Weigh 300g of the chicken stock and transfer to a blender.

Turn on to medium speed and add the xanthan gum.

Blend until incorporated, then add the warm roast chicken fat and finally the soy lecithin powder.

Check the seasoning and add a few drops of fresh lemon juice to balance the flavours.

# ROAST CHICKEN STOCK

4kg chicken wings

1 head of celery

3 leeks

3 medium onions

1 head of garlic

100g dried wild mushrooms

500g button mushrooms

1 tablespoon black peppercorns

1 large sprig of thyme

3 bay leaves

Roast the chicken wings in the oven until golden.

Cut the celery, leeks and onion into large dice.

Add the wings to a large saucepan and cover with cold water.

Bring to the boil, skimming off any of the fat.

Add the diced vegetables, garlic, both mushrooms and the peppercorns simmer for 2 hours.

Add the herbs and simmer for another 2 hours.

Remove from the heat and pass through a fine sieve lined with muslin.

Reduce to the desired consistency and taste.

# FISH STOCK

2 medium onions

1 leek

1 bulb fennel

350g dry white wine

3kg good quality white fish bones, such as turbot, halibut or brill

300g button mushrooms

5 garlic cloves

40g fresh parsley

20g fresh tarragon

20g fresh chervil

1 head of celery

Cut the fennel, onions and leek to a large dice.

In a large pan, on a medium heat sweat the onions, leek and fennel until soft.

Add the white wine and turn up the heat slightly.

Bring to the boil.

Add the bones and cover with cold water, leaving the heat on.

Skim regularly to remove any fat or impurities.

Add the celery, mushrooms, garlic and herbs.

Simmer for 20 minutes.

Remove from the heat and leave to rest for 30 minutes.

Pass through a fine sieve lined with muslin.

# SAFFRON SHELLFISH STOCK

*A really lovely stock that can be used for making risotto or finishing pasta sauces*

3kg shells such as lobster, crab or langoustine

Olive oil, for roasting

2 medium onions

1 leek

1 head of celery

2 medium carrots

1 bulb fennel

300g tomatoes, sieved or chopped

350g dry white wine

500g fish stock

5 garlic cloves

40g fresh parsley

20g fresh tarragon

20g fresh chervil

20g thyme

2g saffron

Preheat the oven to 190°C.

Roast the shells in the oven with a little olive oil until golden, set aside.

Cut the onion, leek, celery, carrots and fennel to a medium dice.

In a large saucepan sauté the vegetables with a little olive oil until they start to colour.

Add the tomato.

Add the wine and bring to the boil.

Add the shells, then the fish stock and cover with cold water.

Bring up to the boil and turn down to simmer.

Skim regularly.

Add the garlic, herbs and saffron.

Simmer for 2 hours.

Remove from the heat and leave to rest for 1 hour.

Pass through a fine sieve lined with muslin.

# PARSNIP AND HAY PURÉE

500g parsnips
2 handfuls of hay
700g water
800g double cream
Fine sea salt
A little xanthan gum (optional)

Preheat the oven to 200°C.

Make a bed of the hay in the base of a large roasting tray.

Wash and trim both ends of the parsnips and cut lengthways.

Lay the parsnips in the hay and pour over 300g of the water.

Cover with foil and bake in the oven until soft (about 2 hours).

When cooked, remove from the oven and lift out the parsnips.

Put the hay, cream and remaining water into a saucepan and bring to the boil.

Pass through a sieve.

In a food processor, blend the hay cream and the parsnips until smooth.

Check for seasoning and add the xanthan.

Pass through a sieve again.

(When storing any purée, place a piece of greaseproof paper over the surface to stop any skin from forming).

# CARROT VADOUVAN PURÉE

500g medium carrots
40g crushed vadouvan spices
2 tins coconut milk
Fine sea salt
Olive oil
1 teaspoon xanthan gum

Peel and cut the carrots into 2cm pieces.

In a medium saucepan sauté the carrots in the olive oil until golden, add the vadouvan spice mix and cook for a further 2 minutes.

Season with the fine sea salt.

Add the coconut milk and enough water to just cover.

Bring to the boil, turn down to a simmer and cook until the carrots are tender.

Blend until smooth.

Add the xanthan gum and check the seasoning.

Pass through a fine sieve.

# CELERIAC AND HAZELNUT PURÉE

2 medium celeriac
2 banana shallots
A large sprig of thyme
150g hazelnut oil
Fine sea salt
Olive oil
1 teaspoon xanthan gum

Peel and dice the celeriac and the banana shallots.

In a medium saucepan, sauté the shallots for 1 minute, then add the celeriac.

Stir until well caramelised and golden.

Add the thyme, then season.

Add enough water just to cover and cook until the celeriac is tender.

Transfer to a blender and blend until smooth.

While the machine is running, add the hazelnut oil and the xanthan gum.

Pass through a fine sieve and adjust the seasoning.

# FERMENTED VEGETABLES

*This method of preserving and the following recipe can be used for most vegetable and herb ferments.*

*It's extremely important that when handling the ingredients or equipment for fermentation that everything is sterilised and ideally wear disposable gloves (we use latex powder-free gloves to minimise the risk of any unwanted bacteria).*

## FERMENTED BABY GEM STALKS

Pack baby gem lettuce stalks in a clean, sterilised Kilner jar (the type with a flip top and a rubber seal).

Zero the weighing scales and pour in enough cold water to cover.

Calculate 2% of the weight of the water and add this in fine sea salt (500g water would be 10g salt).

Seal the jar and leave in a warm dark place for 4 days.

(This is how long we leave the gem stalks at the restaurant but it's all down to personal taste; if you want the ferments to have a more acidic taste, leave for longer).

Open the jar after 2 days to release any build-up of $CO_2$.

After 4 days, transfer the jar to the fridge.

Unopened, these will keep chilled for 4 months.

Once opened, use within 6 weeks.

## FERMENTED GREEN STRAWBERRIES

Pack green strawberries in a clean, sterilised Kilner jar (the type with a flip top and a rubber seal).

Zero the weighing scales and pour in enough cold water to cover.

Calculate 2% of the weight of the water and add this in fine sea salt (500g water would be 10g salt).

Seal the jar and leave in a warm dark place for 6 days.

Open the jar every 2 days to release any build-up of $CO_2$.

After 6 days, transfer the jar to the fridge.

Unopened, these will keep chilled for 4 months.

Once opened, use within 6 weeks.

## SOME MORE IDEAS

A few other ferment ideas that we prepare using the same recipe and principal as the above recipes:

- Whole baby gem
- Beetroot
- Fennel
- Seaweeds, especially Kombu
- Chard stalks
- Parsnip
- Carrot
- Celeriac
- Spring onion
- Young pine shoots (spruce tips)
- Hazelnuts
- Walnuts
- Salsify

# PRINCIPLES OF MAKING VINEGAR

*Because acetobacter bacteria need oxygen to work, a container with an open top that can be covered works best, such as a glass jar or a plastic container (nothing metal as it will corrode).*

*A mother vinegar can be purchased from a good health food shop or any brewery specialists (we use raw unfiltered live apple vinegar).*

## BASIC VINEGAR RECIPE

300g live mother vinegar
100g mineral water
500g alcoholic liquid, or one high in sugar

Mix the ingredients together and place in the container.

Cover the top with a breathable material, such as muslin cloth, and fix in place.

Leave the container at room temperature away from sunlight.

The vinegar should be ready in a couple of weeks depending on the temperature of the room (we leave ours at around 19°C). It can take up to a month.

The layer on the top of the vinegar will become slightly thicker, this is normal, move it to one side and taste.

If the vinegar smells like a paint-thinner, discard the whole batch as it has turned rancid (this is extremely rare).

Gently decant the vinegar into clean, sterilised bottles and keep chilled (the vinegar will mellow with age so keeping it chilled will prolong that a little).

Put the mother vinegar left over from the decanting back into a clean plastic or glass container, add a little fresh live vinegar and this is ready for your next batch. You can let this sit at room temperature for up to 3 weeks if not using straight away.

## BIRCH SAP VINEGAR

*This recipe makes great use of the very short season for birch sap and makes a really lovely vinegar.*

300g live, raw apple vinegar
100g mineral water
500g birch sap (available online)

## SOME MORE IDEAS

*Base liquids with a high alcohol/sugar content:*
Cider
Beer/Ale
White/Red wine

*Flavours (added after the decanting stage):*
Elderflower
Vanilla
Tonka
Walnut
Hazelnut
Violet
Mushroom (especially cep)
Raspberry
Strawberry
Blueberry
Garlic, roast or black
Honey

*Herbs:*
Thyme
Tarragon
Rosemary
Sage
Verbena
Basil
Mint (garden, peppermint or spearmint)

# REDCURRANT CORDIAL

1200g redcurrants
500g caster sugar
Juice of 5 lemons
Small splash of water

Place all the ingredients into a pan and bring to the boil.
Turn down the heat and simmer for 5 minutes.
Pass through a J-cloth lined sieve.
Don't push through the sieve as the cordial will become cloudy.
Bottle in sterilised containers and refrigerate.

# WILD ROSE CORDIAL

20 wild roses
1kg caster sugar
600g water
10g fresh lemon juice
Zest of 1 orange

Remove the petals from the wild roses and place them with 350g of the caster sugar in a plastic bowl.
Rub the sugar into the petals, cover the bowl and leave at room temperature for 10 hours.
Place the sugar/rose mix into a stainless steel pan with the remaining sugar and the other ingredients.
Bring to the boil, turn down and simmer for 5 minutes.
Remove from the heat, pass through a sieve and bottle into sterilised jars.

# ELDERFLOWER CORDIAL

10 elderflower heads
1kg caster sugar
2 lemons, sliced very thinly in rounds
630g water
50g citric acid/vitamin C powder

Bring the water and caster sugar to the boil.
Remove from the heat and leave to cool for 15 minutes.
Add the lemon slices and the elderflowers and then the citric acid.
Cover and leave to infuse for 12 hours.
Strain through a sieve and bottle.

# AVOCADO ICE CREAM

100g sugar
100g dry white wine
50g glucose
80g water
1 lemon, juiced
80g milk
2 avocados

Bring the wine, glucose, milk and sugar to the boil.

Remove from the heat and leave to cool.

In a food processor, blend the avocados and the cooled milk mixture.

Pass through a fine sieve and finish with lemon juice and seasoning.

Churn in an ice cream machine as per manufacturer's instructions.

# TRUFFLE HONEY ICE CREAM

*A great ice cream to serve with a creamy soft cheese such as Bath soft or Brillat-Savarin.*

500g semi-skimmed milk
600g double cream
210g egg yolks
50g caster sugar
75g honey
75g truffle honey

Mix together the egg yolks and caster sugar until pale.

Bring the cream and milk to the boil and pour over the yolks, return to the stove and gradually bring up to 82°C.

Remove from the heat and sieve.

Add the two honeys and chill.

Churn in an ice cream machine as per manufacturer's instructions.

(If using a water bath to cook this it needs 85 minutes at 82°C, then agitate the bag several times and chill over ice.)

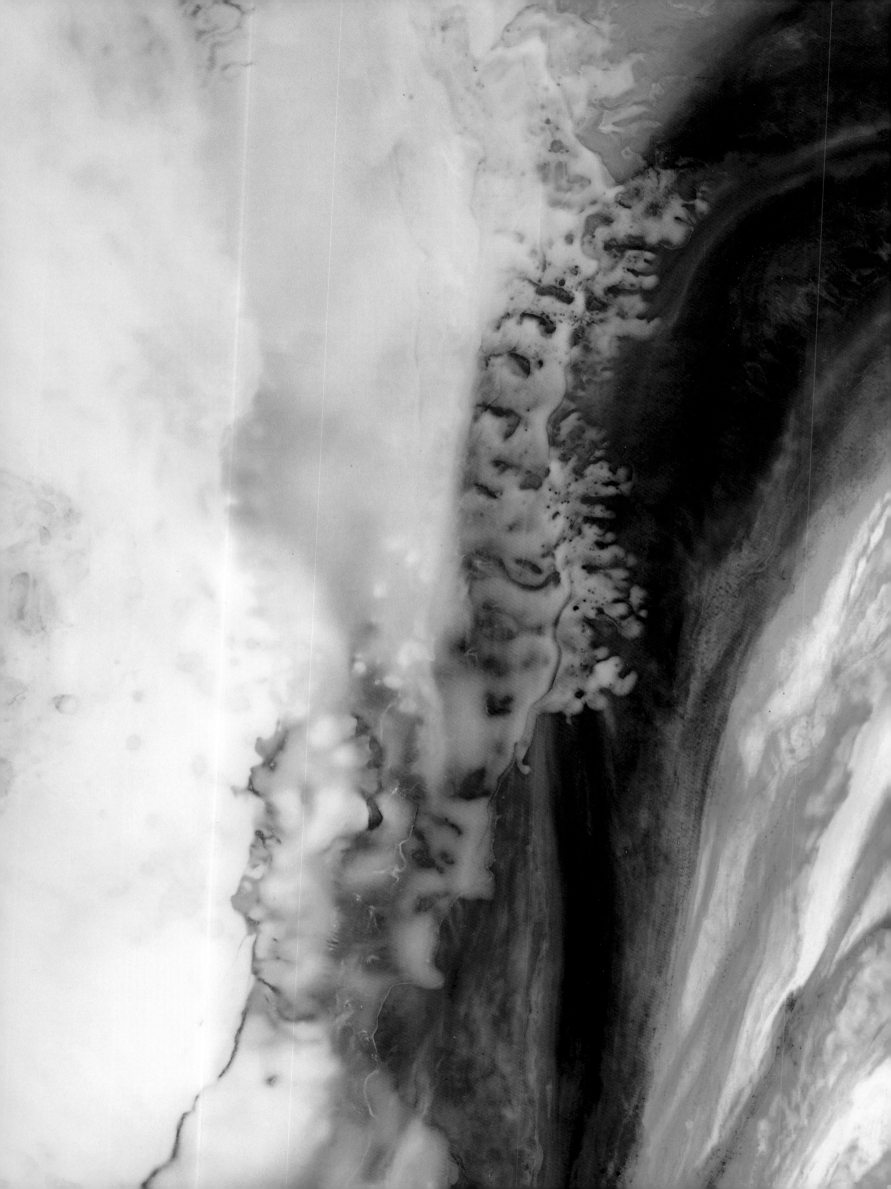

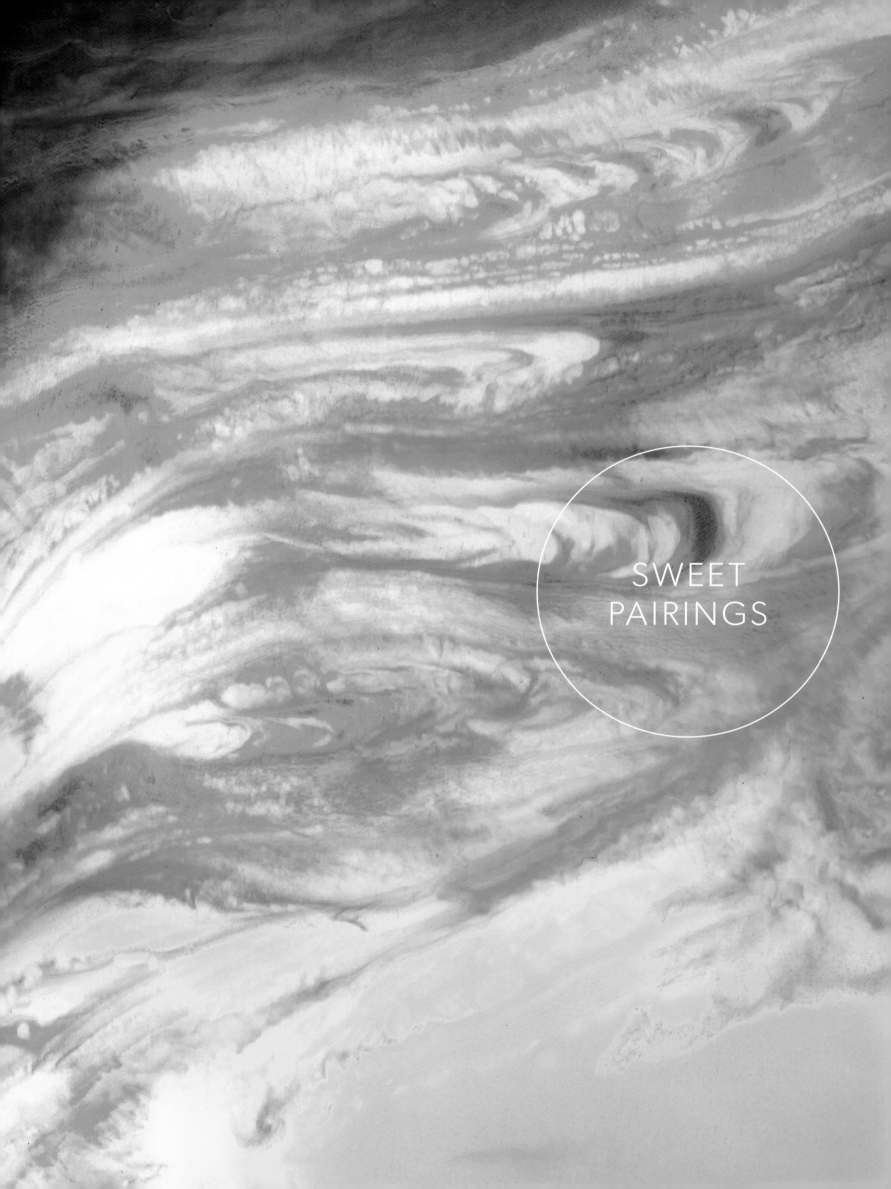

SWEET
PAIRINGS

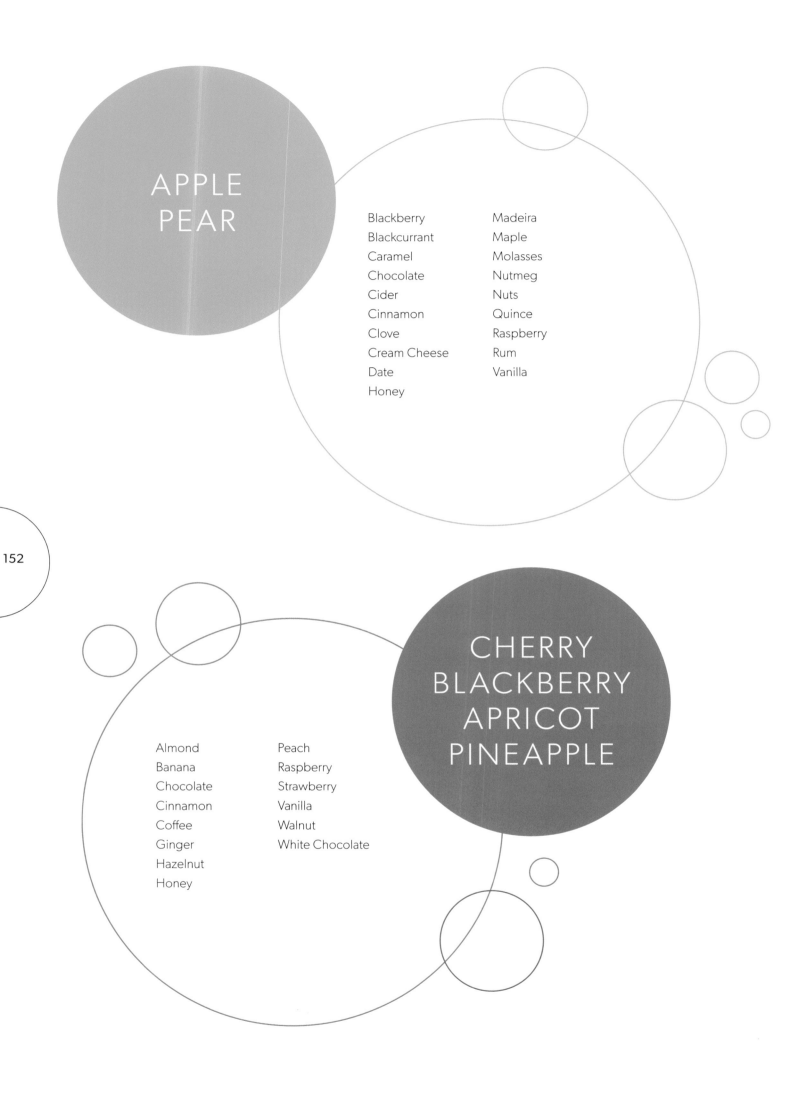

## APPLE PEAR

Blackberry
Blackcurrant
Caramel
Chocolate
Cider
Cinnamon
Clove
Cream Cheese
Date
Honey
Madeira
Maple
Molasses
Nutmeg
Nuts
Quince
Raspberry
Rum
Vanilla

## CHERRY BLACKBERRY APRICOT PINEAPPLE

Almond
Banana
Chocolate
Cinnamon
Coffee
Ginger
Hazelnut
Honey
Peach
Raspberry
Strawberry
Vanilla
Walnut
White Chocolate

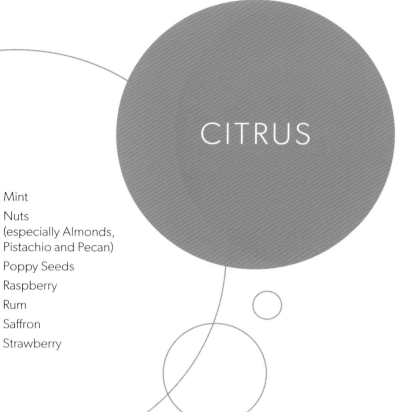

## CITRUS

Anise
Banana
Blackcurrant
Blueberry
Champagne
Cardamom
Chocolate
Cream Cheese
Ginger

Mint
Nuts
(especially Almonds,
Pistachio and Pecan)
Poppy Seeds
Raspberry
Rum
Saffron
Strawberry

153

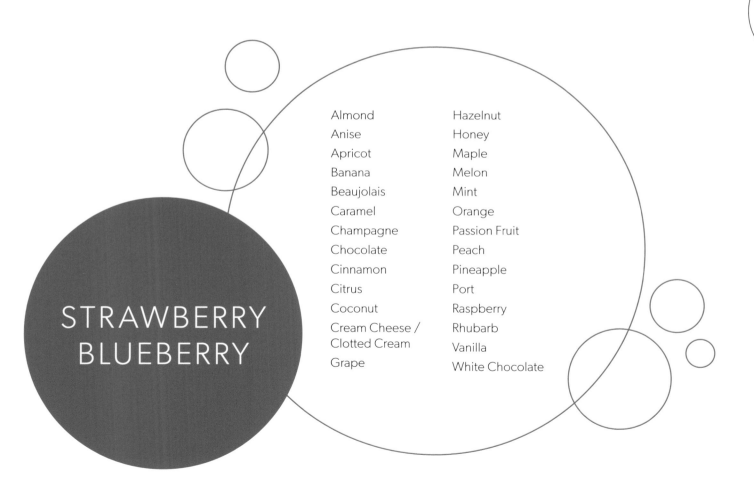

## STRAWBERRY BLUEBERRY

Almond
Anise
Apricot
Banana
Beaujolais
Caramel
Champagne
Chocolate
Cinnamon
Citrus
Coconut
Cream Cheese /
Clotted Cream
Grape

Hazelnut
Honey
Maple
Melon
Mint
Orange
Passion Fruit
Peach
Pineapple
Port
Raspberry
Rhubarb
Vanilla
White Chocolate

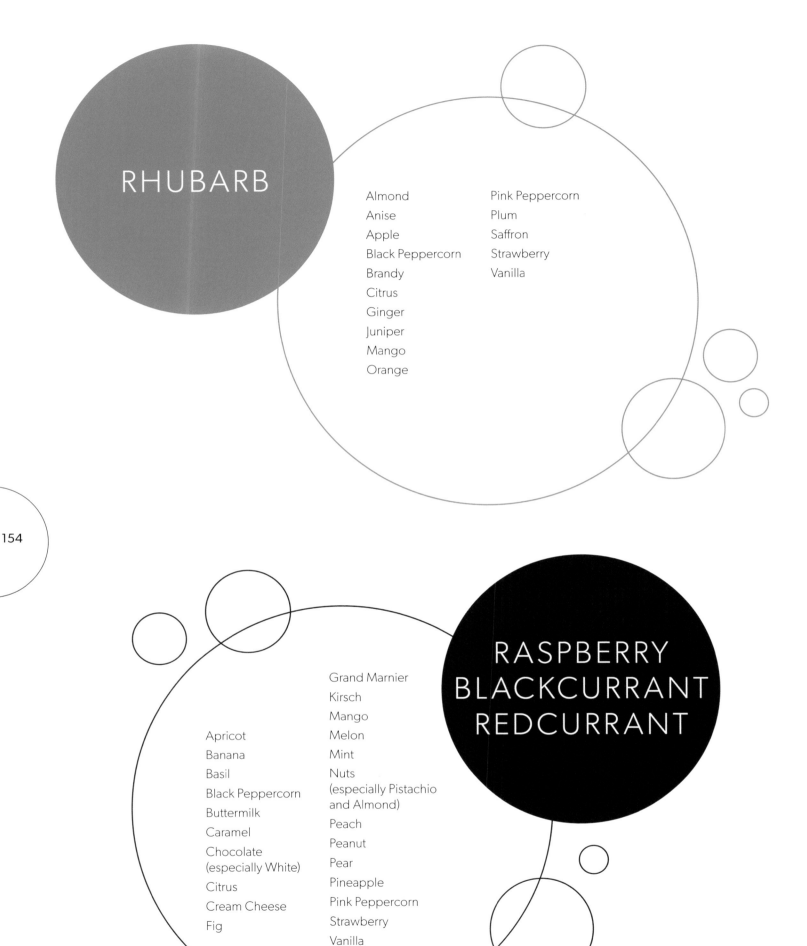

# RHUBARB

Almond
Anise
Apple
Black Peppercorn
Brandy
Citrus
Ginger
Juniper
Mango
Orange

Pink Peppercorn
Plum
Saffron
Strawberry
Vanilla

# RASPBERRY
# BLACKCURRANT
# REDCURRANT

Apricot
Banana
Basil
Black Peppercorn
Buttermilk
Caramel
Chocolate
(especially White)
Citrus
Cream Cheese
Fig

Grand Marnier
Kirsch
Mango
Melon
Mint
Nuts
(especially Pistachio
and Almond)
Peach
Peanut
Pear
Pineapple
Pink Peppercorn
Strawberry
Vanilla

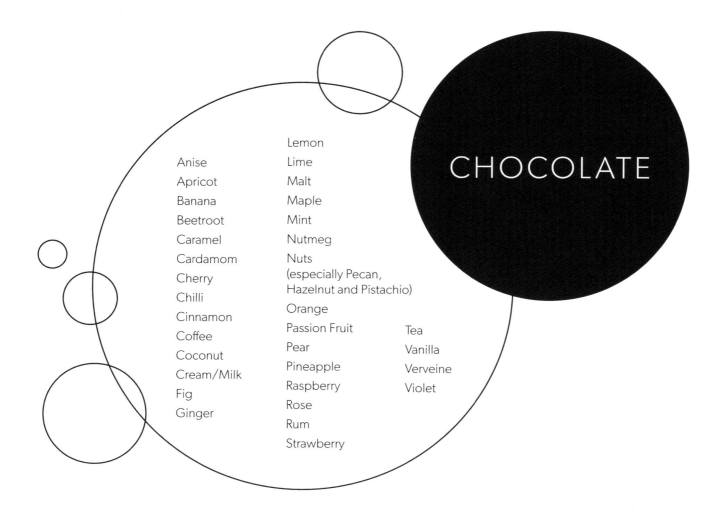

# CHOCOLATE

Anise
Apricot
Banana
Beetroot
Caramel
Cardamom
Cherry
Chilli
Cinnamon
Coffee
Coconut
Cream/Milk
Fig
Ginger

Lemon
Lime
Malt
Maple
Mint
Nutmeg
Nuts
(especially Pecan,
Hazelnut and Pistachio)
Orange
Passion Fruit
Pear
Pineapple
Raspberry
Rose
Rum
Strawberry

Tea
Vanilla
Verveine
Violet

# WHITE CHOCOLATE

Almond
Banana
Bergamot
Blackberry
Cardamom
Cherry
Chocolate
Coconut
Coffee
Lemon
Lime

Olive/Olive Oil
Orange
Pineapple
Raspberry
Rum
Saffron
Strawberry
Violet

"*Invention my dear friends is 93% perspiration, 6% electricity, 4% evaporation and 2% butterscotch ripple*" WILLY WONKA

SWEET
RECIPES

# CHOCOLATE WHISKY
# AND CIGAR BOX ICE CREAM

## CIGAR SUGAR

600g water
200g sugar
1 vanilla pod scraped
1 good quality Cuban cigar
60g malto

Bring the sugar, water and vanilla pod to the boil and set aside.

Bring a medium sized pan of water to the boil, turn down to a simmer and add the cigar (don't boil the cigar).

Leave for 1 minute then carefully remove the cigar, discarding the water.

Blanch the cigar twice, on the second time reserve 150g of the water.

Gently unravel the cigar.

Place the cigar leaves into the syrup and on a gentle heat reduce by two thirds.

Leave to cool.

Remove the leaves from the syrup (the syrup can be put to one side and used to dress the plate).

Dehydrate the leaves for 12 hours until dry and crispy.

Blend the leaves in a food processor to a find powder, add the malto and blend again.

Store at room temperature in a box with a tight-fitting lid.

## WHISKY REDUCTION

450g single malt whisky, such as Balvenie

Reduce over a medium heat until 250g (be careful if doing this over a naked flame as the whisky will flambé if the flame is too hot).

## WHISKY AND VALRHONA CHOCOLATE MOUSSE

110g egg yolks
800g double cream
150g caster sugar
250g whisky reduction
400g Valrhona 50% dark chocolate (or other good quality 50% dark chocolate)

Bring the cream to the boil.

Beat the egg yolks and sugar until pale.

Pour the cream onto the eggs, whisk and return to the stove, stirring all the time.

Gently bring up to 82°C and hold for a couple minutes.

Remove from the stove and strain through a sieve into a clean bowl.

Whisk in the chocolate, making sure it is well incorporated.

Add 200g of the whisky reduction and taste.

Depending on the strength of the whisky you may need to add the remaining 50g of the reduction.

## CIGAR AND WHISKY JELLY

150g cigar water, reserved from the second blanching
100g whisky
50g caster suger
2 gelatine leaves

Soak the gelatine in cold water until hydrated, squeeze out.

Gently warm the cigar water and suger, add the gelatine and whisky, stir until dissolved.

Set in a small box with a tight fitting lid in the fridge.

*continued…*

### CIGAR BOX ICE CREAM

1 litre milk
One quarter of a Cuban cigar
150g double cream
40g oak wood chips
35g high quality untreated cigar box wooden inlays
190g egg yolk
145g caster sugar

Pour the milk into a wide pan and cover with cling film.
Using a smoking gun, light a small amount of the cigar and fill the pan with smoke, leaving for 15 minutes.
Roast the wood chips and cigar inlays in the oven for 10 minutes.
Add to the simmering milk and infuse for 20 minutes.
Pass through a fine seive.
Mix the egg yolk and sugar, then pour the milk on and leave for 10 minutes to infuse.
Return to the stove and cook to 82°C.
Strain and chill.
Churn in an ice cream machine as per manufacturer's instructions.

### MALLEABLE CHOCOLATE JELLY

320g caster sugar
6 eggs
800g dark chocolate (54% is ideal)
300g semi-skimmed milk
8 gelatine leaves, soaked and squeezed

Blend the eggs and sugar in a thermomix at 80°C.
Boil the milk, dissolve the gelatine in it, then add the chocolate.
Add to the eggs.
Carry on blending for a minute.
Set in a lined tray.

### CANELE

*Normally a canele would be made with rum but for this dessert we swapped it for whisky.*

250g milk
1 vanilla pod, scraped
25g diced butter
110g caster sugar
50g whole egg
20g egg yolk
45g plain flour
5g cornflour
25g whisky

Bring the milk, butter, sugar and vanilla to the boil.
Remove from the heat, infuse.
Mix together the yolk, egg, flour and cornflour.
Whisk the milk and the egg mixes together.
Add the whisky.
Cover with cling film and leave chilled overnight.
Next day mix the batter well and pass through a sieve.
Bake in butter or beeswax-greased moulds at 180°C.
Remove from the oven when golden brown, about 20 minutes.

*We serve the canele slightly warm in a cigar box filled with cocoa nibs and a very small amount of cuban cigar smoke inside the box from a small handheld smoker alongside the dessert.*

### TO SERVE

Take a thin slice of the chocolate jelly and let it come to room temperature for a minute (this will make it more malleable).
Make an "S" shape in the centre of the plate.
Place a quenelle of whisky and cigar mousse on one side and a quenelle of the cigar box ice cream on the other, sprinkle with a small amount of cigar sugar, small squares of the jelly and a few drops of the cigar syrup.
Lightly warm the canele for 2 minutes.

160

# MILK CHOCOLATE TART, TONKA ICE CREAM, ESPRESSO FOAM

## MAKES 1 LARGE TART

300g 70% dark chocolate
300g white chocolate
141g unsalted butter

Melt all of the above in a bowl over simmering water (or somewhere warm).

4 large eggs
30g egg yolk
171g caster sugar

Whisk the eggs, yolk and sugar over simmering water with a handheld electric whisk until thick and pale (this is a sabayon) fold into the chocolate and fold in 150g of double cream.
Bake at 140°C for 14 minutes or until the tart has a slight wobble in the centre.
Chill until set.
Serve at room temperature.

## TONKA BEAN ICE CREAM

300g double cream
1 litre semi-skimmed milk
120g egg yolks
260g caster sugar
6 tonka beans, finely grated on a microplane
5g ice cream stabiliser

Whisk together the egg yolks, caster sugar and stabiliser.
Boil the milk, cream and tonka beans.
Add to the egg yolks and sugar.
Return to the stove and gradually bring up to 82°C.
Transfer to a clean, cold pan and leave the tonka to infuse for 20 minutes.
Strain and chill.
Churn in an ice cream machine as per manufacturer's instructions.

## ESPRESSO FOAM

325g cold espresso
125g double cream
75g caster sugar
2 pressed, soaked gelatine leaves
1 x 500ml syphon with 1 x $N_2O$ charger

Heat 50g of espresso, add sugar and gelatine and dissolve.
Off the heat, add the rest of the cold espresso and the cream.
Pass through a chinois and charge in the syphon with the $N_2O$.
Shake well.
Chill for at least 6 hours before use.

# PBJ: ICED PEANUT PARFAIT, MORELLO CHERRY, CORNFLAKE MILK AND TOASTED BRIOCHE

## ICED PEANUT PARFAIT

### STAGE 1: ITALIAN MERINGUE

3 egg whites
100g caster sugar
50g glucose
25g water

Place the sugar, glucose and water in a pan and mix until well incorporated making sure the sides of the pan are clean from sugar.
Using a thermometer, cook to 121°C.
Place the whites in a clean, grease-free bowl for an electric mixer.
When at 115°C start to whip the whites.
Pour the boiling sugar onto the whites on high speed and whip until cold.

### STAGE 2: SABAYON

3 egg yolks
3 whole eggs
100g sugar
50g glucose
25g water

Place the glucose, sugar and water and mix well (as above).
Cook the sugar to 121°C.
Place the whole eggs and egg yolks in a clean grease-free bowl for an electric mixer and turn on medium.
Pour the boiling sugar onto the egg mixture, when the sugar has completely incorporated turn the machine up gradually to high speed and whip until cold.

*Bowl 1*
170g smooth peanut butter
120g double cream

Mix until smooth.

*Bowl 2*
375g double cream

Semi-whip the cream and chill until needed.

Remove the peanut butter and cream mix from the fridge.
Fold in the cold meringue, then the semi-whipped cream, then the cold sabayon.
Pour into moulds and freeze.

## PEANUT BRITTLE

150g caster sugar
15g glucose
100g unsalted peanuts

Cook the sugar and glucose to a light caramel.
Add the peanuts.
Empty onto a lined tray and cool.
Blend in a food processor until a fine powder.
Dust a 2mm-thick layer of powder onto a lined tray and bake in a preheated oven on 170°C until golden (about 6 minutes).
Leave to cool and break into shards.
Keep at room temperature in an airtight box for up to 3 weeks.

*continued…*

## MORELLO CHERRY SORBET

500g morello cherry purée
50g glucose
150g caster sugar (maybe a little more to taste)
1 leaf of gelatine soaked

Heat 100g of the cherry purée with the glucose and the caster sugar.
Add the gelatine and stir until dissolved.
Remove from the heat.
Add the rest of the purée and pass through a sieve.
Chill.
Churn in an ice cream machine as per manufacturer's instructions.

## MORELLO CHERRY JELLY

200g morello cherry purée (we use Boiron)
1½ gelatine leaves, soaked in cold water
50g caster sugar

Heat 50g of the morello cherry purée and caster sugar, add the gelatine and stir until dissolved.
Remove from the heat and whisk in the remaining purée.
Transfer to a plastic container and chill until set.
Cut with a warm knife.

## TOASTED BRIOCHE ICE CREAM

4 slices of brioche, toasted both sides
300g double cream
1 litre semi-skimmed milk
120g egg yolks
260g caster sugar

Boil the cream and the milk and add onto the yolks and sugar.
Return to the stove and heat to 82°C for 8 minutes.
Break up and add the toasted brioche, then blend.
Strain and chill.
Churn in an ice cream machine as per manufacturer's instructions.

## CORNFLAKE MILK PANNA COTTA

100g cornflakes
150g semi-skimmed milk
350g double cream
50g caster sugar
2½ gelatine leaves, soaked in cold water

Toast the cornflakes in a preheated oven at 180°C for 6 minutes.
Bring the cream, milk and sugar up to a simmer.
Remove from the heat.
Squeeze any excess water from the gelatine and stir into the cream until dissolved.
Add the toasted cornflakes and leave to infuse for 20 minutes.
Strain through a fine sieve.
Pour into moulds and set in the fridge.

# ICE CREAM, CREAM, CUSTARD

## THICK ANGLAISE

250g semi-skimmed milk
75g double cream
1 split and scraped vanilla pod
80g egg yolks
60g caster sugar

Boil the cream, milk and vanilla pod.
Pour onto the yolks and sugar, whisk return to the pan and cook gently, stirring until slightly thickened, sieve and leave to cool.

## VANILLA MOUSSE

250g thick anglaise
100g double cream
50g caster sugar
3 leaves gelatine
500g whipped double cream

Warm the 100g of double cream and the sugar and add the softened gelatine then whisk into the thick anglaise.
When cold, fold in the double cream and chilled mascarpone foam.

## MASCARPONE FOAM

250g mascarpone
1 gelatine leaves
50g caster sugar
130g water
1 scraped vanilla pod

500ml syphon with 1x N$^2$O charger

Dissolve the caster sugar in the water and vanilla. gently warm with the gelatine until melted.
Whisk onto the mascarpone until smooth and sieve.
Charge with the N$^2$O, shake well and chill for at least 4 hours before use.

## DEHYDRATED MILK

475g full-fat milk
50g glucose

Whisk together the milk and glucose over a low heat.
Bring the temperature up to 80°C and with a hand held blender froth the milk.
Gently collect the foam from the top and carefully spoon onto a lined dehydrator tray.
Dry on 63°C for 2 hours or until dry and crispy.
Store in an airtight container.

## VANILLA ICE CREAM

500g semi-skimmed milk
500g double cream
5 vanilla pods scraped
155g egg yolks
150g caster sugar

Beat the egg yolks and caster sugar until pale.
Boil the milk, cream and the split and scraped vanilla pods.
Pour onto the yolks and whisk.
Return to the pan and, while stirring, bring up to 82°C.
Hold at 82°C for 4 minutes, remove from the heat and pass through a sieve.
Chill.
Churn in an ice cream machine as per manufacturer's instructions.

## GOLD TOP ICE CREAM

800g full-fat Jersey milk
70g caster sugar
100g condensed milk
18g glucose
1 gelatine leaf, hydrated and squeezed

Reduce 750g of the milk and the sugar to 550g in weight.
Add the condensed milk and glucose, then the gelatine, then the reserved milk.
Whisk.
Strain and chill.
Churn in an ice cream machine as per manufacturer's instructions.

# PEAR TREE

## PEARS

4 baby pears
400g caster sugar
500g water
1 vanilla pod split

Peel the pears.
Heat together the sugar water and vanilla, poach the pears lightly until soft.
Alternatively vac pac the pears and the syrup, poach in a 65°C water bath for 25 minutes, then chill the opened bags in iced water.

## BIRCH SYRUP POWDER

30g birch syrup
50g dark chocolate (54%)
70g malto

Melt the birch syrup and the dark chocolate together, cool slightly.
Transfer into a cold stainless steel bowl and whisk in the malto.
Transfer to a container with a tight-fitting lid.

## SMOKED PEAR WOOD ICE CREAM

950g whole milk
75g pear wood chips
(available from suppliers of smokers and wood chips)
100g double cream
190g egg yolks
145g caster sugar

Preheat the oven to 170°C and roast the wood chips for 12 minutes.
Beat the egg yolks and caster sugar in a bowl until pale.
Boil the milk and cream and pour onto the yolks.
Add the wood chips.
Leave for 10 minutes to infuse.
Strain through a fine sieve.
Return to the stove and bring up to 82°C.
Hold at 82°C for 4 minutes.
Remove from the heat and pass through a sieve.
Chill.
Churn in an ice cream machine as per the manufacturer's instructions.

## BRANCHES

10 whole stalks of chervil, leaves removed
35g egg white
100g caster sugar
45g Horlicks malt drinking powder
45g bitter cocoa powder (80-90%)

Whisk together the egg whites and the sugar until only just incorporated.
Mix together the cocoa powder and Horlicks.
Dip the chervil stalks into the egg white and coat with the cocoa powder.
Line a dehydrator tray with greaseproof and dry at 35°C until crisp and branch-like.

## CELERIAC BARK

120g honey
110g water
6 pieces of thinly-sliced celeriac

Lightly caramelise the honey, add the water (a little at a time) to stop the cooking, being careful as this will spit.

Leave on the side to cool.

Blanch the thin slices of celeriac in lightly sugared water for 10 seconds and refresh in iced water.

Drain and add to the honey liquor.

Leave for 4 hours.

Dry on a lined tray in a dehydrator at 52°C for 8 hours.

The branches and the bark can be prepared beforehand and stored in an airtight container.

## MARQUISE

150g good quality 70% chocolate
(we use Valrhona or Weiss)
250g caster sugar
150g egg yolks (pasteurised)
60g good quality bitter cocoa powder (80%)
550g double cream
330g melted unsalted butter
A small pinch of salt

Melt the chocolate over simmering water and keep warm.

Semi-whip the double cream in a clean bowl and chill.

Melt the butter to lukewarm and add the cocoa powder, stirring until there are no lumps.

Whisk the egg yolks, salt and caster sugar in an electric mixer until tripled in size.

Turn the machine down to slow and add the butter/cocoa mix, then the melted chocolate, then the semi-whipped cream.

Mix until well incorporated.

Chill until needed.

The marquise will last for 4 days in the fridge and can also be frozen.

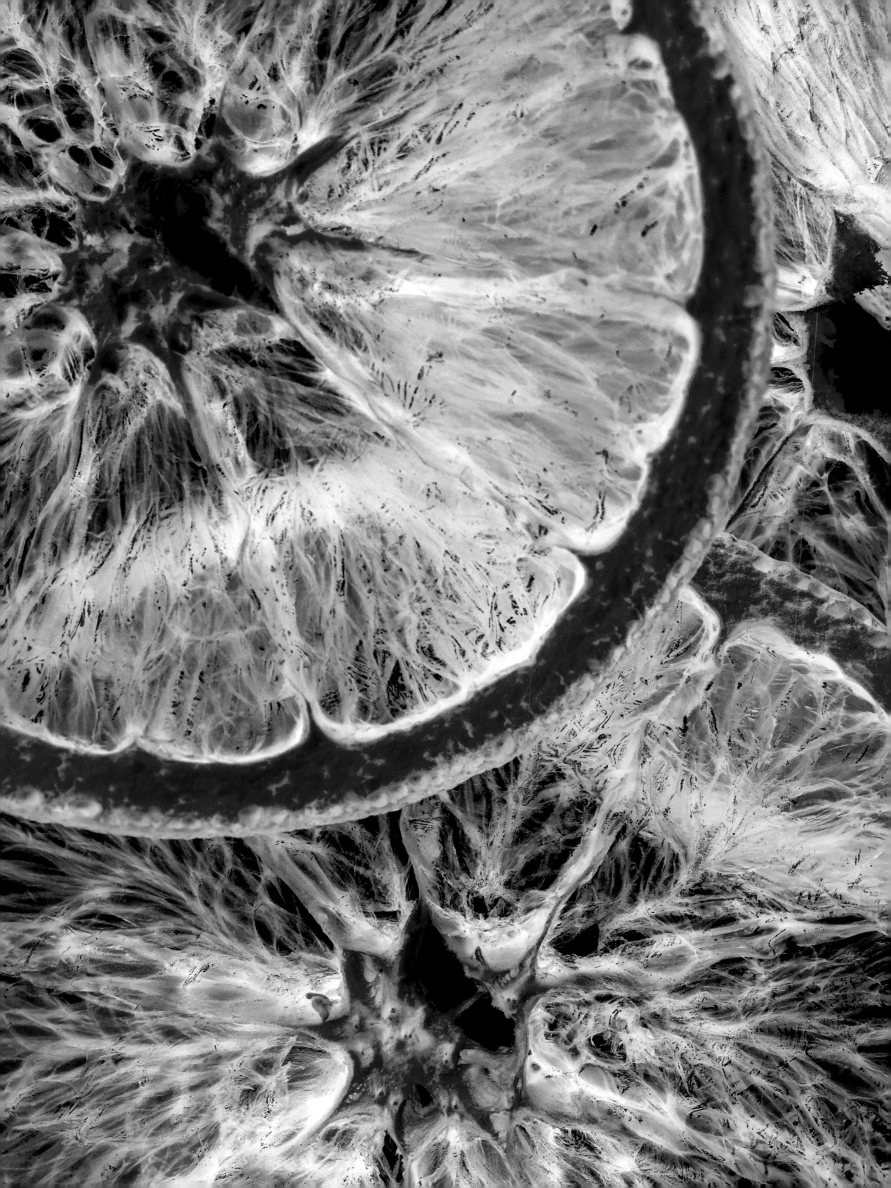

# TONKA AND LEMON DOUGHNUTS

## DOUGHNUTS

500g white flour
65g sugar
10g salt
2 tonka beans, finely grated
15g fresh yeast
4 eggs
155g water
125g soft butter
Grated zest of 2 lemons

## SUGAR COATING

150g caster sugar
1 tonka bean, finely grated

Add all the ingredients except the butter on a machine with a paddle attachment.

On a slow speed, mix all the ingredients until incorporated.

Add the butter in 20g pieces one at a time.

Cover with cling film and prove in the fridge until doubled in size.

On a floured work surface knock the dough back for 5 minutes.

Shape the doughnut with the palms of your hands.

(At this point the doughnuts can be frozen)

Leave to prove at room temperature on a lightly oiled tray until double in size.

Fry at 170°C until golden one side, carefully turn over and repeat.

Remove from the oil and drain on a paper towel to remove any excess oil.

Roll in the tonka sugar and fill with the lemon curd.

## LEMON CURD

4 medium eggs
4 medium egg yolks
205g caster sugar
4 unwaxed, untreated lemons, zested and juiced
230g butter, diced and kept cold
400g whipped double cream

Over a pan of lightly simmering water, in a stainless steel bowl, whisk the eggs, yolks and sugar until thickened.

Remove from the heat and whisk in the butter a little at a time.

Leave to cool slightly.

Fold in the cream.

Gently transfer to a plastic container with a tight fitting lid and keep chilled until needed.

# TONKA, RASPBERRY, HONEYCOMB AND SILVER

### PANNA COTTA

700 ml double cream
300 ml milk
5 gelatine leaves, soaked and drained
160 g caster sugar
2 tonka beans, grated finely

Heat the cream, milk, caster sugar and grated tonka to 85°C.
Remove from the heat and leave to infuse for 20 minutes.
Add the gelatine, whisk until dissolved, pass through a sieve.
Pour into moulds and chill until set.
When completely set, dip the mould into warm water for 20 seconds and with a warm side knife run the tip around the inside of the mould.
Turn upside down and remove the pannacotta (they can be left in their moulds until needed).

### RASPBERRY SORBET

700g raspberry purée
85g glucose
200g caster sugar
2 gelatine leaves, soaked in cold water and squeezed out
5g sorbet stabiliser
8 raspberries, halved, to serve

Take a third of the raspberry purée and warm, add the glucose and caster sugar, mix until dissolved.
Add the gelatine and dissolve.
Whisk into the remaining two-thirds of cold purée (we do this to keep the freshness and colour of the sorbet).
Taste and add more sugar if needed.
Blend in the stabiliser and pass through a sieve.
Churn in an ice cream machine as per the manufacturer's instructions

*continued…*

## HONEYCOMB

160g caster sugar
60g golden syrup
180g glucose
40g water
20g bicarbonate of soda
A shallow pan lined with greaseproof paper

Place everything except the bicarbonate of soda in a pan and mix together well.

The next steps need to be done relatively quickly and carefully.

On the heat, using a sugar thermometer, bring the mixture up to 148°C.

Turn the heat off.

At 148°C sprinkle in the bicarbonate of soda and whisk for 10 seconds, making sure it is absorbed well (being very careful as it will start to rise and be very hot).

Gently, yet quickly, tip the honeycomb into the prepared lined tray and leave to cool completely.

When cold the honeycomb can be broken up and stored in an airtight container.

## TOFFEE AND TONKA FOAM

300g caster sugar
500g double cream
170g semi-skimmed milk
3 tonka beans, finely grated
1 litre syphon with 2 x $N_2O$ chargers

Place the sugar into a pan and slowly cook until a golden caramel.

Carefully deglaze the pan with the other ingredients (at this point the caramel will go solid, as the mixture gets hotter the caramel will slowly dissolve while whisking).

Pass through a sieve and leave to cool slightly.

Fill the syphon and charge with the $N_2O$.

Chill for at least 5 hours before use.

## SILVER

150g white chocolate, melted over simmering water
3 edible silver transfer sheets

Using a pastry brush, paint the melted white chocolate over the silver transfer sheets, place them on a tray and chill until set.

Break up into erratic shapes and sizes.

Store in a box with a tight-fitting lid in the fridge until needed.

# VIOLET BEAUREGARDE

*"Good heavens, girl!" shrieked Mrs Beauregarde suddenly staring at Violet,*
*"What's happening to your nose? It's turning blue!", screamed Mrs Beauregarde,*
*"Your nose is turning as blue as a blueberry!"*

## BUBBLEGUM PANNA COTTA

350ml double cream
150ml milk
2½ gelatine leaves, soaked and drained
80g caster sugar
6 drops of bubblegum essence

Warm the cream, milk and caster sugar, remove from the heat and add the squeezed gelatine leaves.
Dissolve, stirring with a whisk.
Add the bubblegum essence with a pipette.
Pass and pour into moulds.
Chill until set.

## VIOLET CARAMEL

100g Texturas azuleta sugar
125g fondant
70g glucose
70g Patisomalt or isomalt

Dissolve the fondant, glucose and add the Patisomalt.
Cook to 155°C and pour onto a baking mat (being very careful as this will be very hot).
Leave to cool slightly.
Sprinkle with Texturas azuleta and dehydrate at 52°C for 5 hours.
Leave to cool at room temperature.
Blend in a Thermomix.
Bake in a thin layer at 120°C until melted.
Leave to cool.
Break into desired sizes and shapes.
Store in an airtight container until needed.

## BLUEBERRY MERINGUE

300g blueberry Boiron purée
180g cold water
12g egg white powder
200g caster sugar
12g gelatine

Hydrate the egg whites with the cold water for 20 minutes.
Warm a small amount of the blueberry purée and dissolve the gelatine in it.
Whisk into the remaining blueberry purée.
Whisk the whites and slowly add the blueberry and gelatine mix.
Pipe and dehydrate at 55°C for 6 hours or until crisp.

## BLUEBERRY FOAM

250g blueberry purée
100g caster sugar
1 gelatine leaf, soaked in cold water
500ml syphon with 1 x $N_2O$ charger

Lightly warm the blueberry purée with the sugar.
Add the gelatine leaf and stir until dissolved.
Check for sweetness.
Pass through a sieve.
Place the purée into the syphon gun and charge with the $N_2O$.
Shake well for 30 seconds.
Chill for at least 4 hours before use, to set.

*continued...*

## BLUEBERRY MARSHMALLOWS

125g caster sugar
15g glucose
4 gelatine leaves, soaked in cold water
40g egg whites
125g blueberry purée
A few grains of salt
Cornflour for dusting

Heat the sugar and glucose to 117°C.
Whisk the whites with few grains of salt and slowly pour in the sugar.
Warm a small amount of the purée and use to dissolve the gelatine, add to the rest of the purée then add to the whites.
Whip on medium speed until cold.
Pipe onto a tray dusted with cornflour and chill until set.

## BLUEBERRY PAPER

350g Boiron blueberry purée
60g caster sugar
5g xanthan gum

Blend all the ingredients together and spread onto a Silpat.
Dehydrate on 52°C for 12 hours or until dry.
Store or in airtight container until needed.

## BLUEBERRY SORBET

500g blueberry purée
50g glucose
150g caster sugar (maybe a little more to taste)
1 gelatine leaf, soaked

Heat 100g of the blueberry purée with the glucose and the caster sugar.
Add the gelatine and stir until dissolved.
Add the rest of the purée and pass through a sieve.
Chill.
Churn in an ice cream machine as per manufacturer's instructions.

## TO SERVE:

1 pack of popping candy

Lightly dress one corner of the plate with a little popping candy.

# BANOFFEE

## MASCARPONE FOAM

500g mascarpone
2 gelatine leaves
100g caster sugar
260g water
2 vanilla pods, scraped
1 litre syphon with 2 x $N_2O$ chargers

Dissolve the caster sugar in the water and vanilla, gently warm with the gelatine until melted.
Whisk onto the mascarpone until smooth, then sieve.
Pour into the syphon and charge with the $N_2O$, shake well and chill for at least 4 hours before use.

## ROAST BANANA GELATO

3 ripe bananas
60g egg yolks
150g caster sugar
500g semi-skimmed milk
3g ice cream stabiliser

Roast the bananas with their skins on until black and starting to burst, about 20 minutes.
Leave to cool, peel and discard the skins.
Boil the milk.
Whisk the egg yolks and caster sugar together until pale, and pour on the milk, whisk and return to the stove.
Gradually bring the temperature up to 82°C.
Remove from the heat and transfer to a clean bowl.
With a hand blender, incorporate the cooked bananas and ice cream stabiliser.
Leave to cool.
Churn in an ice cream machine as per the manufacturer's instructions.

## CARAMEL SAUCE

100g caster sugar
50g glucose
250g double cream
1 cinnamon stick

Cook the sugar and glucose to a golden colour and deglaze with double cream and a cinnamon stick.
Bring back to a simmer and dissolve all the caramel.
Sieve and chill.

## GRANOLA

120g Demerara sugar
80g honey
40g golden syrup
80g butter
160g oats
130g dried grated coconut
275g mixed nuts including pistachio, hazelnuts, almonds and macadamia

Gently heat together the butter, honey and golden syrup, then add to the other ingredients and mix well.
Bake in the oven until golden, about 25 minutes, 170°C.

## CARAMELISED BANANA

16 slices of banana
Small amount of caster sugar

Sprinkle each slice of banana with a small amount of caster sugar and caramelise with a blowtorch.

## MILK CHOCOLATE POWDER

50g Valrhona milk chocolate (30%)
100g Texturas malto

Melt the chocolate over simmering water (or in a microwave) and scrape into a clean, large stainless bowl.
Slowly add the malto until it has absorbed all the chocolate.
(This will make more than you need, it will keep in an airtight box for up to 2 weeks and can be used in other desserts).

# WHITE

## WHITE CHOCOLATE MOUSSE

125g milk
Zest of 1 lime
2½ gelatine leaves, soaked in cold water
225g white chocolate
250g double cream, semi-whipped

Heat the milk, add the lime zest.
Remove from the heat, add the gelatine.
Pour onto the white chocolate and whisk until smooth, leave to cool.
When cold, fold in the whipped cream and set in the fridge.

## WHITE CHOCOLATE CRUMB

*Stage 1*
45g skimmed milk powder
40g strong white flour
12g cornflour
45g caster sugar
55g unsalted butter, melted

*Stage 2*
30g milk skimmed milk powder
100g white chocolate, melted

Preheat oven to 150°C.
Mix all the Stage 1 ingredients together in a bowl, mix well.
Pour onto a lined tray and bake until a light golden colour.
Transfer to a bowl and add the Stage 2 ingredients, mix well.
Chill and mix every 10 minutes until set.
Pulse the white chocolate crumb in a food processor to get it really fine.

## WHITE CHOCOLATE, ISOMALT

250g isomalt sugar
125g liquid glucose
90g white chocolate

Put the isomalt and glucose in a pan and, using a sugar thermometer, bring it up to 157°C.
Remove from the heat and add the chocolate, then pour onto a non-stick baking mat.
Leave to cool and set.
When set break up into pieces and blend into a fine powder.
Preheat the oven to 160°C.
Dust the powder on a tray lined with a silicone mat and melt in the oven for 2 minutes.
Remove and let the chocolate cool slightly before breaking up into pieces.

## LYCHEE SORBET

400g Boiron lychee purée
100g water
1 gelatine leaf, soaked in cold water
5g sorbet stabiliser
75g caster sugar (lychee purée can be quite sweet so start at 75g, you may need a little more)

Heat the water and sugar and add the softened gelatine.
Stir until dissolved.
Add to the lychee purée and, using a hand blender, incorporate the sorbet stabiliser.
Churn in an ice cream machine as per manufacturer's instructions.

*continued...*

## COCONUT FOAM

500g Boiron coconut purée
1½ gelatine leaves, soaked in cold water
85g caster sugar
(maybe a touch more depending on the purée)
500ml syphon with 1 x N$^2$O charger

Warm 100g of the coconut purée with the sugar.
Add the softened gelatine, mix until dissolved.
Whisk in the remaining purée, check the sweetness.
Pass through a sieve and fill the syphon.
Charge with the N$^2$O and shake well for 30 seconds.
Leave refrigerated for at least 3 hours before use.

## ITALIAN MERINGUE

100g caster sugar
25ml water
50g egg white
Freeze-dried passion fruit powder

Combine the sugar and water and mix well.
Using a sugar thermometer, cook to 115°C.
On an electric mixer start whisking the whites on high speed.
At 121°C remove the sugar from the heat and pour in a steady slow trickle into the whites, whip until cold.
Spread the cold meringue onto a lined dehydrator tray 5mm thick, sprinkle with the passion fruit powder and dry at 60°C until crispy, about 6 hours.
Break into large pieces and store at room temperature in an airtight box.

## COCONUT LEGO

Lego brick moulds (available online)
200g Boiron coconut purée
40g sugar
1½ gelatine leaves, softened in cold water

Warm half the purée with the sugar, add the softened gelatine and stir until dissolved.
Add the other half of the purée and mix well.
Check the sweetness.
Pass through a fine sieve and pour into Lego brick moulds.
Freeze (it's easier to turn these out frozen and then defrost an hour before needed).

## ROAST LEMON PURÉE

4 lemons
Xanthan gum
150g caster sugar

Preheat oven to 160°C.
Wrap the lemons in foil and bake for 90 minutes.
Remove from the oven, remove from the foil and leave to cool for 20 minutes.
Cut in half and remove the flesh.
Transfer to a blender with any juice from the baking and the sugar and turn on medium.
(The quantity of sugar needed will differ depending on the sharpness of the lemons).
Thicken with a little xanthan gum and pass through a fine sieve.
Store in a the refrigerator until needed.

## APPLE CLOUD

200g unsweetened cloudy freshly pressed apple juice
10g lemon juice
30g water
3 gelatine leaves, soaked in cold water
65g sugar syrup (equal quantities water and caster sugar, boiled and chilled; this can be made in advance in a larger quantity as it can be used in a lot of recipes)

Mix 65g sugar syrup with the apple juice, lemon juice and water.
Warm a little of the juice mix and dissolve the gelatine in.
Add the rest of the juice mix.
Transfer to an electric mixer and whisk on high speed until it becomes a meringue texture.
Fill moulds and chill.

180

# FROZEN YEAST PARFAIT, GRANNY SMITH, TOASTED BRIOCHE ICE CREAM

## FROZEN YEAST PARFAIT

100g milk
60g yeast
10g caster sugar

Gently warm the above ingredients to 37°C and leave in a warm place for 15 minutes.
Gradually heat up to a simmer and remove from the heat.

800g semi-whipped cream
280g egg yolks
220g caster sugar
150g water

Heat the sugar and water to 121°C, pour into the yolks and whisk on medium speed until cold.
Mix the yeast and the yolk mix together and fold in the cream.
Fill moulds and freeze.

## GRANNY SMITH

4 Granny Smiths apples
80g caster sugar
20g unsalted butter
A few drops of fresh lemon juice

Peel and finely dice the Granny Smiths.
Melt the butter over a medium heat, add the sugar, then the apples.
Stir to incorporate well and cook over a low heat until the apples are half-cooked.
Remove from the heat and stir in the lemon juice.
Chill until needed.

## TOASTED BRIOCHE ICE CREAM

4 slices of brioche, toasted both sides
300g double cream
1 litre semi-skimmed milk
120g egg yolks
260g caster sugar

Boil the cream and the milk and add onto the yolks and sugar.
Return to the stove and heat to 82°C for 8 minutes.
Break up and add the toasted brioche, then blend.
Strain and chill.
Churn in an ice cream machine as per manufacturer's instructions.

# BATH SOFT, PICKLED RAISINS, BURNT GRANNY SMITH, TRUFFLE HONEY ICE CREAM

## BATH SOFT CHEESE

2 slices of Bath soft cheese per person

## PICKLED GOLDEN RAISINS

375g maple syrup
500g white wine vinegar
250g golden raisins

Bring the maple syrup and the vinegar to the boil and pour onto the raisins, leave for 24 hours before using.

## BURNT GRANNY SMITH PURÉE

6 Granny Smiths
Water, as needed
A few grains of sea salt
Half a teaspoon xanthan gum

Preheat the oven to 190°C.
Roast the apples, every 30 minutes remove the tray from the oven and mush the apples together scraping from the sides, roast until a very dark caramel colour.
Remove from the oven and transfer to a blender.
Add enough water to loosen the cooked apples and blend until smooth.
Season with a very small amount of salt.
Thicken with the xanthan gum.
Pass through a fine sieve.
Store in the refrigerator until needed.

## WHITE TRUFFLE HONEY ICE CREAM

210g egg yolks
50g caster sugar
600g double cream
500g semi-skimmed milk
75g honey
75g white truffle honey

Whisk the egg yolks and caster sugar together until pale.
Bring the cream and milk to the boil and pour over the yolks, return to the stove and gradually bring up to 82°C.
Remove from the heat and pass through a sieve.
Add the two honeys and chill.
Churn in an ice cream machine as per the manufacturer's instructions.

## CRUMIEL

50g Texturas Crumiel

Preheat the oven to 180°C.
Sprinkle the Crumiel onto a lined tray and bake in the oven until melted.
Leave to cool until cool enough to handle and, as you remove the warm Crumiel from the tray, stretch and bend it into the desired size and shapes.
Keep in an airtight box at room temperature until needed.

# SHERBET FOUNTAIN (C.1942)

## LIQUORICE ICE CREAM

380g semi-skimmed milk

170g soft panda brand organic liquorice (available from health food shops)

40g egg yolks

70g caster sugar

120g double cream

200g water

In a medium saucepan heat the water, liquorice, milk and cream to a simmer, turn down the heat and stir on a frequent basis (this will burn if not stirred) until the liquorice has melted.

Pour onto the egg yolk mixture.

Return the pan and cook to 80°C.

Pass through a fine sieve and chill.

Transfer to an ice cream machine and churn as per the manufacturer's instructions.

## SHERBET

200g icing sugar

45g Texturas fizzy

Blend both ingredients together as fine as possible and pass through a fine sieve.

Kept at room temperature in an airtight box, the sherbet will keep for 3 weeks.

## VANILLA ICE CREAM

250g semi-skimmed milk
250g double cream
3 vanilla pods
80g egg yolks
75g caster sugar

Split the vanilla pods lengthways and scrape the seeds out.
Put the pods, seeds, milk and cream in a pan and on to boil.
Whisk the egg yolks and sugar until pale.
Pour on the boiling vanilla mixture and whisk.
Return to the stove and cook to 80°C.
Pass through a sieve (the vanilla pods can be washed, dried and used to flavour sugar) and chill.
Churn in an ice cream machine as per the manufacturer's instructions.

## 'CONE'

6 wafer ice cream cones
10g Texturas malto

In a food processor blend the cones to a fine powder, add the malto and store in an airtight box until needed.

## FLAKE POWDER

30g good quality 30% milk chocolate
60g Texturas malto

Over simmering water, melt the chocolate, remove from the heat and mix in the malto until it is a uniform lump-free powder.

## VANILLA FOAM

250g mascarpone
1 gelatine leaves
50g caster sugar
130ml water
2 vanilla pods, scraped
500ml syphon with 1 x N$^2$O charger

Dissolve the caster sugar in the water and vanilla, gently warm with the gelatine until melted.
Whisk onto the mascarpone until smooth.
Sieve and place in the syphon.
Pour the syphon with the N$^2$O charger, shake well and chill for at least 4 hours before use.

# QUEEN OF HEARTS

## STRAWBERRY TART

*For this you will need a picture of the Cheshire cat, printed on edible paper. This image is available online and can be printed using a printer set up with edible ink and rice paper, available from pastry specialists online.*

## STRAWBERRY JELLY/JUICE

500g ripe strawberries

55g caster sugar

3g citric acid

1½ gelatine leaves, soaked and squeezed to remove excess water

Combine the strawberries, sugar and citric acid in a round bottom bowl over simmering water.

Cover with cling film and leave to simmer for 2 hours.

Strain and chill.

Weigh out 200g of the strawberry juice, reserving the remaining juice.

Lightly warm 100g of the juice, add the soaked gelatine and stir until dissolved.

Remove from the heat and stir in the remaining 100g.

Pour into a small plastic tub and chill until set.

Cut into 5mm squares with a warm knife.

## COMPRESSED STRAWBERRIES

8 ripe, firm strawberries

60g strawberry juice (from previous recipe)

6 fresh verveine leaves

Slice the strawberries lengthways 3mm thick and place in a vac pac bag with the verveine and strawberry juice.

Vac pac on full vacuum and chill for 2 hours before using.

(Alternatively mix the ingredients together and chill for 2 hours).

## SWEET PASTRY CRUMB

250g plain flour

100g unsalted butter, in pieces, at a cold room temperature

1 large egg, beaten

100g icing sugar

1 vanilla pod, split and scraped

Preheat the oven to 180°C.

In a mixer, blend the flour, vanilla pod and icing sugar.

Blend in the butter, piece by piece.

When all the butter has been incorporated, blend in the beaten egg.

Empty onto a lined tray and bake in the oven at 180°C until golden (about 12 minutes).

Remove from the oven and leave to cool.

When cool, blend to a fine crumb and store at room temperature in an airtight box.

(This will keep for up to 2 weeks).

## WILD STRAWBERRY TART SORBET

500g Boiron wild strawberry purée

100g glucose

50g caster sugar

2 gelatine leaves, soaked and squeezed to remove excess water

75g sweet pastry crumb

Warm 100g of the strawberry purée, add the glucose, sugar and gelatine.

Stir until dissolved.

Remove from the heat and mix into the rest of the strawberry purée.

Pass through a sieve and chill.

Churn in an ice cream machine as per the manufacturer's instructions.

If using a regular ice cream machine, remove when the sorbet is churned and fold in the pastry crumb by hand.

If using a Pacojet, churn the sorbet once, freeze for an hour then churn again with the pastry crumb.

*continued…*

### DEHYDRATED STRAWBERRY SLICES

15 strawberries, large, ripe yet firm
9g extra virgin olive oil
5g icing sugar

Slice the strawberries lengthways in 2mm slices.
Place in a bowl, sprinkle in the icing sugar and olive oil and gently mix.
Dry on a lined dehydrator tray at 52°C until crispy (about 6-8 hours).
(These can be kept at room temperature in an airtight box for 1 week).

### CARAMEL PASTRY CREAM

*Custard*
375g milk
150g double cream
2 vanilla pods, scraped
160g caster sugar
80g egg yolks
25g cornflour

Boil the milk, cream and vanilla pods.
Whisk onto the other ingredients.
Return to the heat and cook until slightly thickened.
Pour onto a lined tray and cover with a piece of greaseproof paper to stop a skin forming.
Leave to cool.

*Caramel*
100g caster sugar
100g double cream

Cook the sugar to a light golden colour.
Deglaze with the cream.
Whisk until all the sugar has dissolved.
Remove from the heat, pass through a sieve and leave to cool.

When the caramel and the custard are both cold, fold them together and chill.
Store in an airtight container in the fridge until needed.

### MASCARPONE PARFAIT

250g mascarpone
1½ gelatine leaves, soaked in cold water and squeezed
50g caster sugar
3 tablespoons water
1 vanilla pod, scraped

Over a low heat, dissolve the sugar and vanilla in the water, add the softened gelatine and stir until dissolved.
Remove from the heat and whisk into the mascarpone.
Pass through a fine sieve and pour into moulds.
Chill until set, unmould and cut with a warm knife.

### WHITE CHOCOLATE TRANSFERS

250g good quality white chocolate
1 cocoa butter transfer sheet
(available online or specialist pastry shops)

Melt the white chocolate over simmering water and pour onto the cocoa transfer on a lined tray.
Spread thinly and evenly with a palette knife and chill until set.
When set, remove the transfer sheet and break the chocolate to the desired shape and size.
Store in the fridge in an airtight box.

### STRAWBERRY ITALIAN MERINGUE

100g caster sugar
25ml water
50g egg white
Freeze-dried strawberry powder, to sprinkle

Dissolve the sugar in the water.
Using a sugar thermometer, cook to 115°C.
Whisk the whites in an electric mixer on high speed.
When the sugar reaches 121°C, remove from the heat and pour in a steady, slow trickle into the egg whites.
Whip until cold.
In a lined dehydrator tray, spread the cold meringue in a layer 5mm thick.
Sprinkle with the strawberry powder.
Dry at 63°C until crisp (about 6 hours).
Break into desired size pieces and store at room temperature in an airtight box.

# EGG YOLK AND APRICOT BRANDY ICE CREAM

500g egg yolk
750g sugar syrup (50/50)
150g water
120g apricot brandy

Bring the water, apricot brandy and sugar syrup to the boil.

Pour onto the egg yolks and whisk.

Return to the pan and gently bring up to 82°C, stirring all the time (this can also be done in a water bath).

Strain and chill.

Churn in an ice cream machine as per the manufacturer's instructions.

# TONKA BEAN ICE CREAM

300g double cream
1 litre semi-skimmed milk
120g egg yolks
260g caster sugar
6 tonka beans, finely grated on a microplane
5g ice cream stabiliser

Whisk together the egg yolks, caster sugar and stabiliser.

Boil the milk, cream and tonka beans.

Add to the egg yolks and sugar.

Return to the stove and gradually bring up to 82°C.

Transfer to a clean, cold pan and leave the tonka to infuse for 20 minutes.

Strain and chill.

Churn in an ice cream machine as per manufacturer's instructions.

# BURNT CHOCOLATE ICE CREAM

1350g semi-skimmed milk
1 vanilla pod, split in half and scraped
300g caster sugar
290g egg yolks
300g milk chocolate, ideally about 30% cocoa solids

Place the chocolate in a metal saucepan and put directly onto a medium heat, stirring with a spatula; we want this chocolate to burn, so carefully cook the chocolate until it is black.

Remove from the heat and leave to cool for 15 minutes.

Whisk the egg yolks and caster sugar until pale.

Boil the milk and vanilla pod, pour onto the pale yolks and whisk.

Return to the stove and cook to 82°C.

Remove from the heat and add the warm, burnt chocolate.

Transfer to a cold bowl.

Leave to infuse for 1 hour.

Strain and chill.

Churn in an ice cream machine as per manufacturer's instructions.

# BURNT HONEY ICE CREAM

500g full-fat milk
250g good quality honey
80g egg yolks
300g double cream
5g ice cream stabiliser

Caramelise the honey to a light golden caramel.

Bring the cream and milk to the boil and use this to deglaze the honey to stop it cooking. Whisk until dissolved.

Pour onto the egg yolks, whisk, return to pan and cook to 82°C.

Blend in the ice cream stabiliser.

Strain and chill.

Churn in an ice cream machine as per manufacturer's instructions.

# CIGAR BOX ICE CREAM

1 litre milk
One quarter of a Cuban cigar
150g double cream
40g oak wood chips
35g high quality untreated cigar box wooden inlays
190g egg yolk
145g caster sugar

Pour the milk into a wide pan and cover with cling film.

Using a smoking gun, light a small amount of the cigar and fill the pan with smoke, leaving for 15 minutes.

Bring the milk to the boil.

Roast the wood chips and cigar inlays in the oven for 10 minutes.

Add to the milk and infuse.

Mix the egg yolk and sugar, then pour the milk on and leave for 10 minutes to infuse.

Return to the stove and cook to 82°C.

Strain and chill.

Churn in an ice cream machine as per manufacturer's instructions.

# GOLD TOP ICE CREAM

1600g full-fat Jersey milk
140g caster sugar
200g condensed milk
35g glucose
2 gelatine leaves, hydrated and squeezed

Reduce 1500g of the milk and the sugar to 1100g in weight.

Add the condensed milk and glucose, then the gelatine, then the reserved milk.

Whisk.

Strain and chill.

Churn in an ice cream machine as per manufacturer's instructions.

# HAY ICE CREAM

40g hay
650g milk
120g soft dark brown sugar
300g single cream
180g egg yolks
20g soft dark brown sugar
480g hay milk

Roast the hay in the oven for 12 minutes in between two trays.
Bring the milk up to a simmer and submerge the hay.
Infuse for 20 minutes, then strain.

Add a little water to the 120g soft dark brown sugar and cook to a temperature of 150°C.
Remove from the heat and add the single cream (this will spit so be careful).
Place on the stove and whisk until the caramel has dissolved, pour onto the egg yolks and 20g sugar and whisk.
Add the sieved hay-infused milk.
Return to the pan and slowly heat to 82°C, stirring with a wooden spatula.
Chill.
Churn in an ice cream machine as per manufacturer's instructions.

# HAZELNUT ICE CREAM

130g hazelnuts with husks removed
450g full-fat milk
80g caster sugar
70g egg yolks

Blend the hazelnuts in a food processor and toast in the oven for 15 minutes.
Whisk the egg yolks and sugar until pale.

Boil the milk and pour onto the yolks.
Return to the stove and heat to 82°C.
Remove from the heat and pass through a sieve.
Add the warm toasted hazelnuts.
Chill overnight.
Pass through a fine sieve (the hazelnuts can be used for the hazelnut cake recipe).
Churn in an ice cream machine as per manufacturer's instructions.

# TOASTED CROISSANT ICE CREAM

6 croissants, halved and toasted both sides
300g double cream
1 litre semi-skimmed milk
120g egg yolks
260g caster sugar

Whisk the egg yolks and sugar until pale.
Boil the cream and the milk and add onto the yolks and sugar.
Return to the stove and heat to 82°C for 8 minutes.
Break up and add the toasted croissants, then blend.
Strain and chill.
Churn in an ice cream machine as per manufacturer's instructions.

# TOASTED BRIOCHE ICE CREAM

4 slices of brioche, toasted both sides
300g double cream
1 litre semi-skimmed milk
120g egg yolks
260g caster sugar

Whisk the egg yolks and sugar until pale.
Boil the cream and the milk and add onto the yolks and sugar.
Return to the stove and heat to 82°C for 8 minutes.
Break up and add the toasted brioche, then blend.
Strain and chill.
Churn in an ice cream machine as per manufacturer's instructions.

# SMOKED WOOD ICE CREAM

1 litre lightly-smoked milk
150g double cream
70g wood chips
(we use three oak wood biscuits from the Bradley smoker)
190g egg yolk
145g caster sugar

Roast the wood chip biscuits in the oven at 180°C for 10 minutes.
Whisk the egg yolks and sugar until pale.
Add to the boiling milk and infuse.
Pour onto the egg yolk/caster sugar mix and leave to infuse for 20 minutes.
Pass through a fine sieve.
Return to the stove and heat to 82°C.
Strain and chill.
Churn in an ice cream machine as per manufacturer's instructions.

# MINT ICE CREAM

330g milk
100g double cream
75g fresh mint/spearmint/peppermint
100g egg yolks
85g caster sugar

Beat the egg yolks and sugar until smooth.
Boil the milk and cream then add the mint and infuse for 5 minutes.
Strain through a sieve.
Pour onto the yolks and sugar, return to the pan and slowly bring up to 80°C while stirring with a spatula.
Strain and chill.
Churn in an ice cream machine as per manufacturer's instructions.

# BITTER CHOCOLATE SORBET

1000g water
500g sugar
500g semi-skimmed milk
150g Valrhona 50% dark chocolate
150g good quality bitter cocoa powder

Heat everything gently to 75°C.
Pass through a fine sieve and chill.
Churn in an ice cream machine as per manufacturer's instructions.

# YOGURT SORBET

500g natural yogurt
60g caster sugar
100g glucose

Warm the yoghurt and add the glucose and caster sugar.
Bring gently up to 65°C then sieve.
Cover and leave overnight in a cool place to ripen.
Churn in an ice cream machine as per manufacturer's instructions.

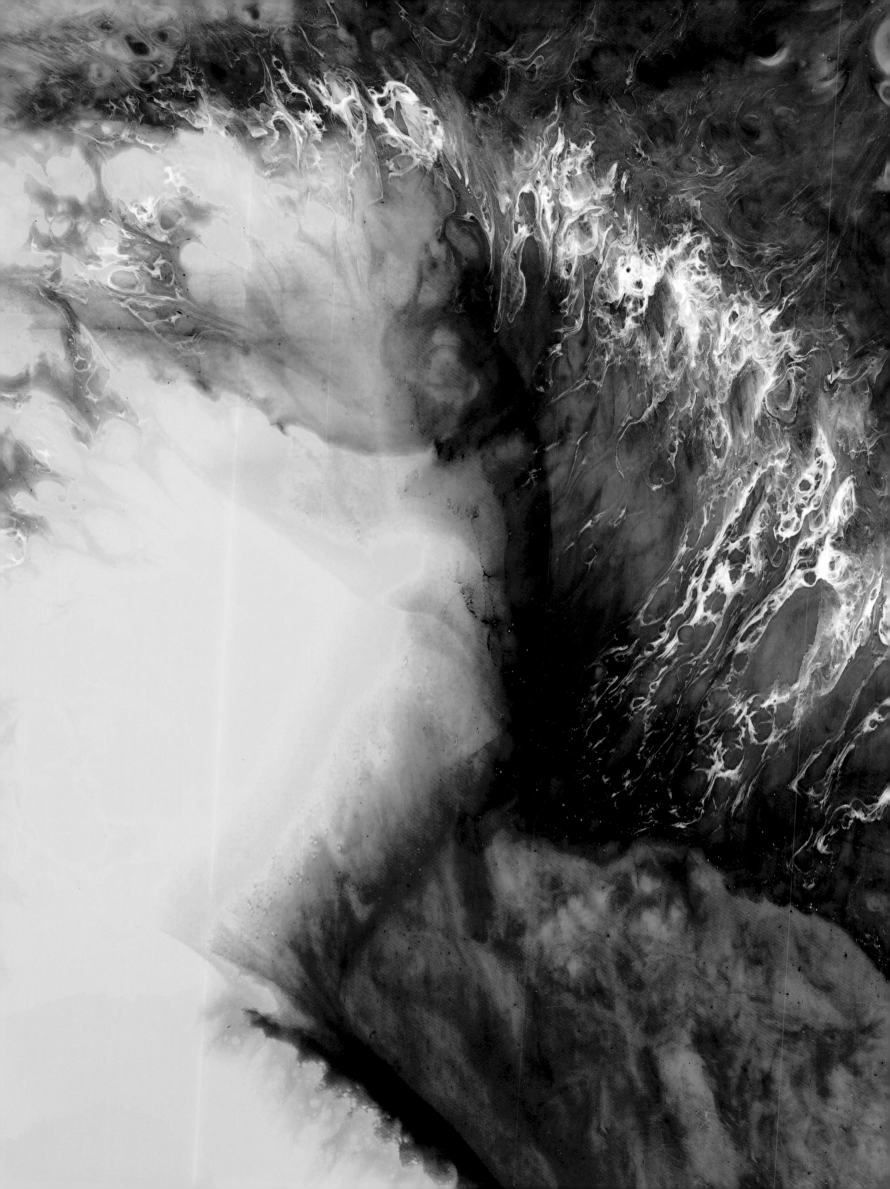

PETIT FOURS

# MACARONS

*For a filling, the caramelised white chocolate mousse is great. Here I've included my favourite, burnt toast ganache.*

310g icing sugar
310g ground almonds
115g egg whites
A few drops of your chosen food colouring

Sift the icing sugar and the ground almonds together, add the egg whites and colour and beat to a fine smooth paste.

300g caster sugar
75g spring water
115g egg whites, whisked

Bring the sugar and water to 117°C and pour onto the whisked egg whites.

Whip until cold.

Beat one third of the meringue into the almond mixture, then gently fold in the rest.

Pipe and bake at 150°C until the macaron has a firm base and when touched has no movement (about 17 minutes).

Remove from the oven and cool.

## BURNT TOAST GANACHE

450g double cream
450g white chocolate
120g burnt toast
125g butter
50g olive oil
4g salt

Boil the cream, then add the toast and blend.

Add half the white chocolate and whisk, then add the other half.

Blend in the butter, olive oil and salt.

# MADELEINES

1 teaspoon ground cinnamon
160g flour
1 teaspoon baking powder
50g ground almonds
160g butter, plus 50g, softened, for greasing
15g honey
4 eggs
170g sugar
100g Boiron passion fruit coulis, reduced down to
4 teaspoons concentrated passion fruit syrup
2 scooped-out passion fruits
Butter, for greasing

Sieve together the cinnamon, flour, baking powder and ground almonds.

Melt the 160g butter and add the honey, keep warm.

Whisk the eggs and sugar together.

Fold flour mix and the passion fruit into the egg mix.

Whisk in the butter and honey mix.

Chill for 24 hours before baking.

Grease the madeleine moulds with the remaining butter and half fill with batter.

Bake in a preheated oven on 190°C until golden brown.

Leave to cool for a few minutes before unmoulding.

# BLOOD ORANGE MARSHMALLOWS

250g caster sugar

25g glucose

9 gelatine leaves, soaked in cold water

80g egg whites

250g blood orange Boiron purée

5g citric acid

Heat the sugar, glucose and a few drops of water to 117°C.

Whisk the whites and fold the sugar in.

Warm a small amount of the blood orange purée and dissolve the gelatine into it, then add the rest of the purée.

Add this to the whites, then the citric acid and whip on high speed until cold.

Pipe onto a lined tray and chill until set.

# FARLEY'S RUSK AND MALT MARSHMALLOW

120g water

10g glucose

225g caster sugar

130g slightly caramelised malt extract

9 gelatine leaves

80g egg whites

1 packet of original Farley's rusks

Heat the liquid malt extract over a low heat until slightly caramelised, keep warm.

Blend the rusks to a powder in a food blender and pass through a fine sieve.

Store in a container with a tight-fitting lid until needed.

Start to beat the whites in an electric food mixer with a whisk attachment.

Bring the water, sugar and glucose to 117°C.

Add to the beaten whites in a slow stream.

Soak the gelatine and melt it in the warm caramelised malt.

Add to the meringue and beat until cold.

Pipe out onto a tray lined with greaseproof paper dusted with some of the Farley's rusk powder.

After piping, dust the tops with the remaining rusk powder.

# FRUIT JELLY BABIES

80ml tonic water

40g gelatine

Cooking spray oil

350g fruit purée, such as morello cherry, blackcurrant or mandarin

200g caster sugar

110g clear honey

50g golden syrup

40g gum arabic

6g vanilla seeds

Grease the jelly baby moulds with the cooking spray.

Soak the gelatine in the tonic water and heat it to 50°C.

Combine the sugar, honey, golden syrup, gum arabic and 200gr of the fruit purée.

Bring to the boil and add the gelatine tonic mix.

With a Bamix blend in the remaining 150g fruit purée and vanilla.

Pour into moulds and leave to set.

# PÂTÉ DE FRUIT

940g fruit purée, such as mandarin, passion fruit or blood orange

60g caster sugar

30g powdered fruit pectin

5g citric/tartaric acid

670g granulated sugar

200g glucose

100ml spring water

Bring the fruit purée to the boil, mix together the caster sugar and the pectin, add, bring back to the boil.

Add the granulated sugar and the glucose and bring up to 108°C on a medium heat, stirring occasionally.

Dilute the citric/tartaric acid in the spring water and whisk into the boiling purée.

Pour into a lined, greased mould and leave out to set.

Chill in the fridge then cut, roll in granulated sugar and leave to air dry.

# CHOCOLATE AND CEP GANACHE TRUFFLE

1kg 70% dark chocolate
1kg double cream
23gr ground cep powder
Good quality cocoa powder, for rolling

Bring the cream and cep powder to a simmer and cook out for a few minutes.
Add to the chocolate and whisk until smooth.
Chill until set.
Shape and roll in the cocoa powder.

# CHOCOLATE AND TONKA FUDGE WITH EDIBLE WRAPPERS

12g sea salt
300g unsalted butter
150g good quality dark chocolate (70%)
720g caster sugar
230g liquid glucose
530g double cream
4 tonka beans, finely grated
Obulato edible starch wrappers

Cook the glucose, sugar and 120ml of water until a light golden caramel.
Add the cream, butter and salt and cook until 118°C on a sugar thermometer.
Remove from the heat and add the chocolate and grated tonka, stirring well.
Pour into a lined tin and chill.
Cut the fudge into required size squares and wrap in the obulato paper.
(This fudge can be wrapped up to 1 day before it is needed).

# BEETROOT WHITE CHOCOLATE AND HERB STONES

600g red beetroot juice
75g caster sugar
1 sprig rosemary
1 sprig thyme
200g double cream
1kg white chocolate, melted
A few grains of salt
200g icing sugar
3g grey and 3g black food colouring powders

Reduce the beetroot juice, sugar, rosemary and thyme to 140g.
Reduce the cream to 140g in another pan and add the two mixtures together.
Fold in 600g of melted white chocolate, mix well and chill.
Melt 400g of white chocolate and add 2g of grey and 2g of black food colouring powders.
Mix in the remaining 2g of food colouring powders with the icing sugar.
Mould the ganache roughly so they resemble stone shapes and chill again.
Dip into the grey chocolate and chill again.
When firm roll into the grey icing sugar.

# CHOCOLATE MARMITE

70g Marmite
50ml water
120g sugar
200g double cream
500g good quality dark chocolate (54%)
Good quality cocoa powder, for rolling

Place the Marmite, water, sugar and double cream in a pan and bring to a simmer.
Remove from the heat and pour onto the chocolate.
Whisk until smooth.
Pour into a plastic container and chill.
When completely set, remove from the fridge and leave to soften slightly.
Roll small pieces in your palms, then roll in the cocoa powder and chill until needed.

# SMOKED WOOD MERINGUE

100g cold smoked egg whites
130ml water
15g dried egg white
170g caster sugar
20g oak chips

With a handheld smoker filled with oak wood chips, cold smoke the egg whites in a container with a tight fitting lid, leave for 10 minutes, then repeat twice.

Bring the water to the boil, add the oak chips and leave to cool.
Infuse for 10 minutes and strain.
In a clean, grease-free electric mixer bowl, whisk the smoked and dried egg whites together on medium speed.
Mix 100g wood-infused water to the sugar and, using a sugar thermometer, cook over a medium to high heat to 120°C.
When the whites are firm, remove the hot sugar from the stove and pour in a steady stream into the whites.
Beat on a high speed until cool.
Transfer the meringue to a piping bag and pipe onto a lined tray.
Dry in a low oven at 90°C for 7 hours (or dry and crisp when cold).

# FISHERMAN'S FRIEND MERINGUE

29 Fisherman's Friends, powdered
170g water
15g powdered egg white
350g caster sugar
200g water

Whisk the water and the egg white in an electric beater for a couple of minutes and leave to hydrate for 10 minutes.
Heat the caster sugar and the water to 121°C and, whilst whisking at a high speed, pour onto the powdered egg mixture, then add the powdered Fisherman's Friends and continue to whisk at high speed until cold.
Pipe onto lined trays and dry out at 110°C for 4 hours.
Serve in Fisherman's Friend packets.

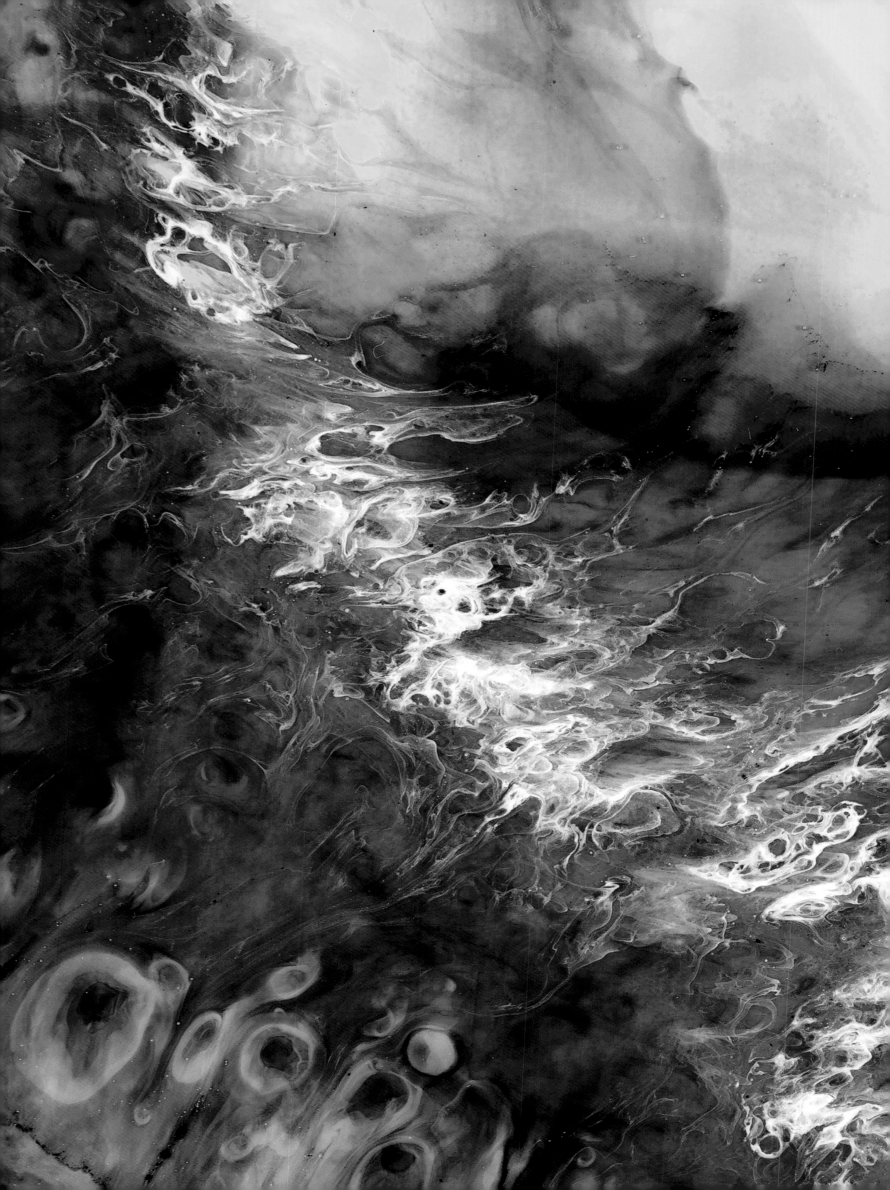

SWEET
BUILDING
BLOCKS

# BREAD AND BUTTER FOAM

160g egg yolks

170g caster sugar

300g semi-skimmed milk, plus extra for blending

300g double cream

2 vanilla pods, split and scraped

6 slices of medium-sliced white bread, buttered with unsalted butter.

Boil the milk and cream with the vanilla pods and pour onto the egg yolks and sugar.

Leave to infuse for 10 minutes, then strain.

Pour onto the buttered bread.

Bake the bread and butter at about 180°C until just set.

Caramelise the top with a little sugar under the grill and leave to cool slightly.

Transfer the bread and butter to the Thermomix and start to blend slowly, adding a little milk until it has the consistency of thick double cream.

Pass through a chinois and load into a syphon, charge with two chargers and chill.

# CITRUS FOAM/JELLY

400g citrus juice (grapefruit, lime and lemon, or a 50/50 lemon and yuzu mix)

300g caster sugar

7 gelatine leaves, soaked in cold water and squeezed out

Warm 120g of the juice with the caster sugar.

Add the soften gelatine and stir until dissolved.

Remove from the heat and add the rest of the juice.

Pass through a sieve.

If using as a jelly, pour into a mould and set in the fridge, cut to the desired shape and size with a warm knife.

If using as a foam, transfer to a 1 litre syphon and charge with 2 x $N_2O$ cartridges, shake well and chill for at least 4 hours before use.

# JERSEY MILK JAM

2 litres Jersey full-fat milk

600g caster sugar

3g bicarbonate of soda

1 vanilla pod, split lengthways and scraped

Bring the milk to the boil.

Add the sugar, bicarbonate soda, vanilla pod and seeds.

Turn the heat down and cook for 45 minutes–1 hour, stirring occasionally, until golden brown in colour with the consistency of caramel.

Remove the vanilla pod, pour into a container and chill.

# LEMON CURD

4 medium sized eggs

4 egg yolks from medium sized eggs

205g caster sugar

4 unwaxed untreated lemons zested and juiced

230g diced cold butter

400g whipped double cream

Over a pan of lightly simmering water, in a stainless steel bowl whisk the eggs, yolks and sugar until thickened.

Remove from the heat and whisk in the diced cold butter a little at a time, leave to cool slightly and fold in the cream, gently transfer to a plastic container with a tight fitting lid and keep chilled until needed.

# CARAMEL PASTRY CREAM

160g caster sugar

150g double cream

375g milk

80g egg yolks

25g cornflour

2 vanilla pods, scraped

Boil the milk, cream and vanilla pods, whisk onto the other ingredients.

Return to the stove and cook until slightly thickened.

Pour onto a lined tray and cover with a piece of greaseproof paper to stop a skin forming.

## CARAMEL

100g caster sugar

100g double cream

Make caramel by cooking the sugar to a light golden colour and deglaze with the cream.

Whisk until all the sugar has dissolved.

Remove from the heat and pass through a sieve.

When the caramel and the thick custard are both cold, fold them together and chill.

Store in an airtight container until needed.

# BUTTERSCOTCH ANGEL DELIGHT

120g unsalted butter

310g muscovado sugar

2g fine sea salt

Half a vanilla pod, scraped

50g double cream

250g milk

2 tablespoons cornflour

180g egg yolk

250g whipping cream, semi-whipped

Bring the butter, sugar, vanilla, salt, double cream and 200g of the milk to the boil and remove from the heat.

In a separate bowl mix the cornflour, the rest of the milk and the egg yolks.

Whisk in half the sauce and mix well, add the rest of the sauce and cook on a medium heat whisking until it starts to thicken and become glossy.

Strain and chill, fold in the semi-whipped cream when cold.

Pour into glasses and set.

## BUTTERSCOTCH SAUCE

170g caster sugar

50g water

2 tablespoons glucose

10g butter

300g double cream

Bring the glucose, water and sugar to the boil and cook until a dark amber caramel colour.

Add the butter and half the cream, bring back to the boil and remove from the heat, whisk in the other half of the cream.

# RICE PUDDING SKIN FOAM

60g pudding rice
600g semi-skimmed milk
3 tablespoons caster sugar
1 tablespoon skimmed milk powder
2 strips of lemon zest
Grated nutmeg
20g butter diced for the top
Extra milk
1 litre syphon with 2 x $N_2O$ chargers

Mix the first six ingredients together and place in an ovenproof dish.

Put the diced butter on top and bake in the oven at 180°C until a brown skin forms (as we are turning this into a foam we need a the skin to be slightly overcooked).

Leave to cool slightly and transfer to a blender, blend until smooth adding some extra milk until the rice has the texture of double cream.

Check for sweetness.

Pass through a sieve and pour into the syphon, charge, shake well and chill for 3 hours before using.

# 30 SECOND SPONGE
# WITH NUT PRALINE PASTES

165g pistachio, almond, walnut or hazelnut paste
6 large eggs
1 egg yolk
120g caster sugar
45g plain flour

Whisk together all the ingredients until smooth and pass through a sieve.

Fill a 1 litre syphon and charge with three $N_2O$ chargers. Chill for 3 hours.

Pierce the bottom of some disposable cups, half fill from the syphon and cook on full power in the microwave for 30 seconds, leave to rest for a few seconds upside down and release from the cups when slightly cooled.

# CARROT CAKE

4 green cardamom pods
8 cloves
1 small cinnamon stick
1 teaspoon grated fresh nutmeg
Small pinch of salt

Lightly toast in a dry pan and blend to a powder.

400g carrots, blanched and puréed
250g milk
300g vegetable oil
320g caster sugar
6 eggs
20g baking powder
150g ground almonds
320g flour

Beat together the eggs and sugar, add the oil, purée and milk, then the flours and spices.

Bake at 190°C for 30-35 minutes.

# PISTACHIO CAKE

50g polenta
200g ground pistachios
50g plain flour
1 teaspoon baking powder
125g extra virgin olive oil
100g unsalted butter, melted and cooled
125g whole egg (about 3 medium eggs)
200g caster sugar
Juice and zest of 1 lemon
Juice and zest of 1 orange

Mix the polenta, pistachios, flour and baking powder.
Add the olive oil and butter.
Beat the eggs and sugar until pale.
Add the olive oil mix.
Then add the juices and zest.
Bake at 160°C for 45 minutes.
The cake should be slightly moist in the middle when checked with a metal skewer.

# TOASTED HAZELNUT CAKE

450g ground hazelnuts
180g whole egg (about 6 medium eggs)
400g caster sugar
400g unsalted butter, softened
100g plain flour
10g baking powder
Juice and zest of two lemons

Preheat oven to 180°C.
In a dry frying pan, gently toss the ground hazelnut over a medium heat until lightly golden.
Using an electric whisk attachment, beat the eggs and sugar until pale.
Add the soft butter and mix until well incorporated.
Fold in the flour, hazelnut flour and baking powder, then lastly the lemon juice and zest.
Pour into a lined tray and bake in an oven at 180°C until lightly golden (about 20 minutes).
Turn out onto a cooling rack and leave to cool.
Cut into the desired shaped size when cold.

# CRUNCHY YOGHURT SPONGE

150g pasteurised egg white
33g caster sugar
30g ground almonds
10g plain flour
40g powdered yoghurt

Blend all the ingredients together until smooth.
Pass through a sieve and transfer to a 500ml syphon.
Charge with one $N_2O$ cartridge and shake well.
Disperse half way up into a disposable plastic cup.
Microwave for 30 seconds on medium power.
Carefully remove from the cup and leave to cool.
Transfer to a lined dehydrator tray and dry on 53°C until crispy (about 6 hours).
Cut into desired sizes and store in airtight box.

# CORNFLAKE MILK PANNA COTTA

100g cornflakes
150g semi-skimmed milk
350g double cream
50g caster sugar
2½ gelatine leaves, soaked in cold water

Toast the cornflakes in a preheated oven at 180°C for 6 minutes.
Bring the cream, milk and sugar up to a simmer.
Remove from the heat.
Squeeze any excess water from the gelatine and add to the cream.
Stir to dissolve.
Add the toasted cornflakes and leave to infuse for 20 minutes.
Strain through a fine sieve.
Pour into moulds and set in the fridge.

# SHORT PASTRY

500g plain flour
290g butter at room temperature
8g fine sea salt
2 medium eggs
22g cold milk
Small pinch of caster sugar

In a bowl, add the plain flour, salt and sugar together and gradually mix in the butter and egg until well incorporated.
Add the milk and knead the dough gently until it starts to come together.
Wrap in cling film and rest in the fridge for at least 3 hours before use (any excess can be frozen).
Remove from the fridge and allow to soften slightly before rolling.
On a floured work surface, roll the pastry to the desired thickness, line the pastry mould and return to the fridge.
Bake blind with greaseproof paper either filled with blind baking beans or coins in a preheated oven at 180°C until golden.

# SWEET PASTRY

200g icing sugar
500g plain flour
4 medium eggs
1 vanilla pod, split and scraped
200g unsalted butter, at room temperature

Sift the icing sugar and flour together.
Beat the eggs.
In a mixer with a paddle attachment, place the flour mixture and the vanilla seeds.
On a slow speed, add the butter 20g at a time until incorporated.
Add the beaten eggs and mix until combined.
Remove from the machine and cover with cling film.
Rest in the fridge for at least 4 hours before use (any excess can be frozen).
Remove from the fridge and allow to soften slightly before rolling.

# MAPLE SYRUP MOUSSE

175g maple syrup
2 softened gelatine leaves
200g cream cheese
200g semi-whipped cream

Heat one third of the maple syrup add the gelatine until dissolved.
Remove from the heat.
Add the rest of the syrup and mix in the cream cheese.
Chill slightly and fold in the whipped cream
Fill moulds and chill to set.

# CARAMELISED WHITE CHOCOLATE MOUSSE

370g semi-skimmed milk
1 vanilla pod, scraped
3 sheets gelatine, soaked and drained
500g melted white chocolate
500g double cream, semi-whipped

Preheat the oven to 190°C.
Place the melted chocolate on a lined try and bake in the oven until golden brown.
Warm the milk and vanilla pod, add the gelatine and dissolve, pour onto the caramelised chocolate and whisk.
Pass through a sieve discarding any white chocolate solids.
Leave to cool.
Gently fold in the cream and chill to set.

# MILK CHOCOLATE FOAM

250g good quality 30% milk chocolate
50g full-fat milk
250g double cream
2½ gelatine leaves soaked and squeezed
1x 500ml syphon gun with 1 x $N_2O$ charger

Bring the cream and milk to simmer, whisk onto chocolate and add the gelatine.
Pass through a chinois.
Fill the syphon gun with the chocolate and tightly seal the top.
Charge with the $N_2O$ and shake well for 20 seconds.
The mousse can be used after 10 minutes resting or kept warm at around 62°C.
This foam can't be chilled or kept.

# FLAVOURED CHOCOLATE AERO

500g milk chocolate (30%)
125g flavoured oil (e.g. pine, almond, pistachio, hazelnut)
1 litre foam canister with 3 x N$^2$O 8g chargers

*For this recipe the foam canister needs to be kept in a warm place (the canister and its parts must be warm before the chocolate and oil mixture is added).*

Completely melt the chocolate and add the flavoured oil with a plastic spatula, making sure it is well incorporated with no lumps.

Add the chocolate into the warm canister and charge quickly three times with the N$^2$O, shaking well between each one.

Carefully and slowly dispense the pressurised chocolate into a lined container with high sides.

From here we can put the box straight in the freezer to set or we can put in a vac pac machine. Turning the machine on will start to pull the chocolate to the top of the box. When it reaches its highest, turn the machine off at the wall leaving the vacuum in the machine.

The chocolate will now set (the colder the room the better).

Leave for at least 3 hours.

Turn the machine back on and release the lid.

# CHOCOLATE MARQUISE

600g double cream
150g egg yolks
250g caster sugar
80g cocoa powder
310g butter, melted
160g 70% dark chocolate, melted

Semi-whip the cream, cover and chill until needed.

Using an electric mixer, beat the egg yolks and sugar until pale and doubled in size, turn the speed down to medium.

Whisk the cocoa powder into the warm butter until smooth and lump free, add to the yolk mixture.

Then add the semi-whipped cream and mix until well incorporated.

Transfer to a plastic box with a tight-fitting lid and chill until set.

213

# WHITE CHOCOLATE, ISOMALT

250g isomalt sugar
125g liquid glucose
90g white chocolate

Put the isomalt and glucose in a pan and, using a sugar thermometer, bring it up to 157°C.

Remove from the heat and stir in the chocolate, then pour onto a non-stick baking mat.

Leave to cool and set.

When set break up into pieces and blend into a fine powder.

Preheat the oven to 160°C.

Dust the powder on a tray lined with a silicone mat and melt in the oven for 2 minutes.

Remove and let the chocolate cool slightly before breaking up into pieces.

Store in an airtight container.

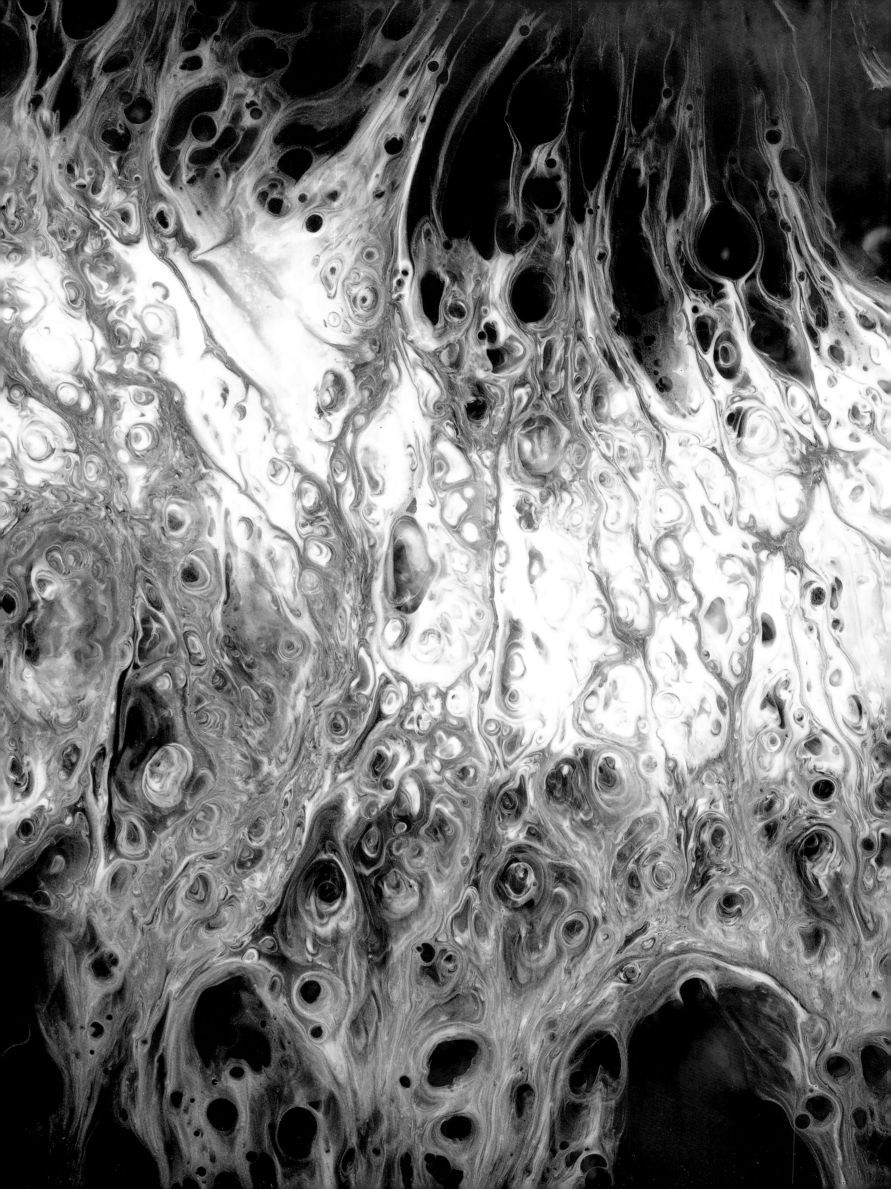

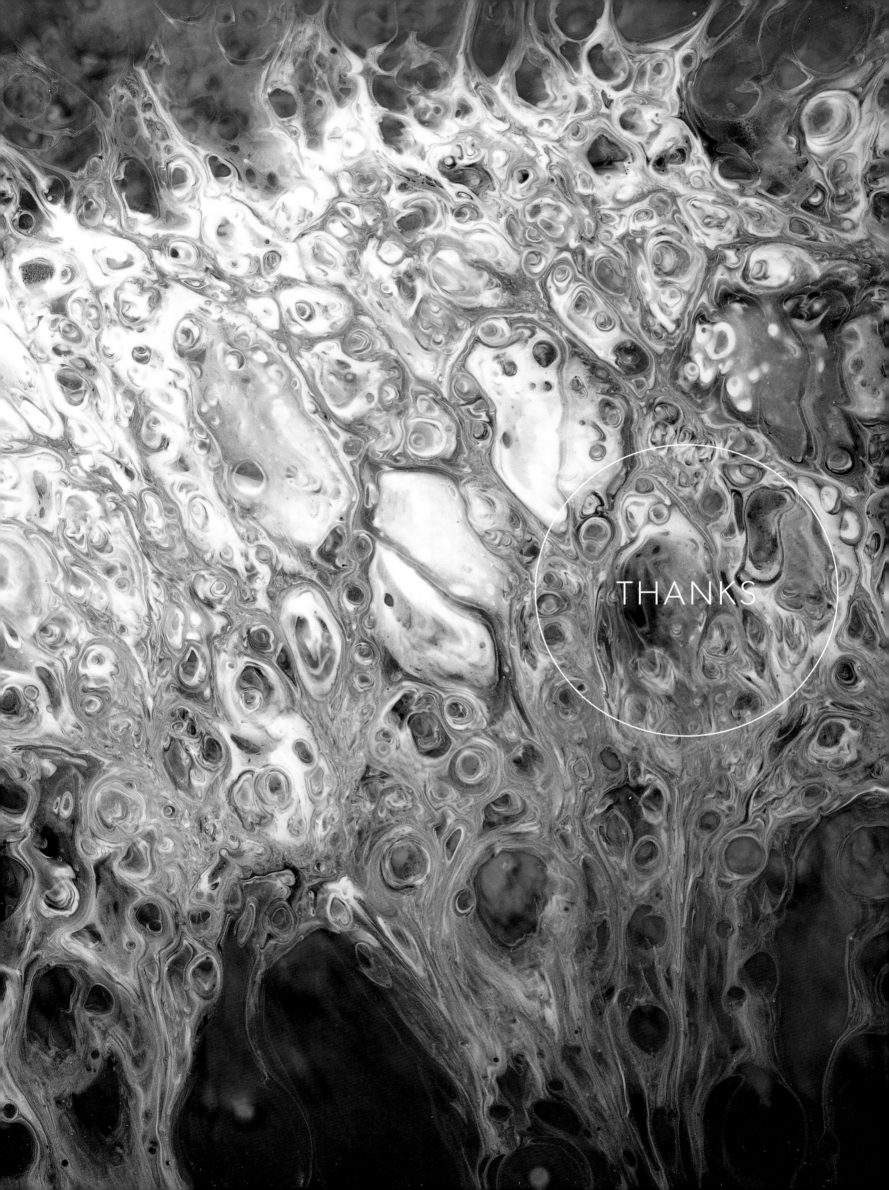

THANKS

# THANKS & ACKNOWLEDGEMENTS

216

Thank you to my family for the support, help and advice you've offered throughout my career.

To the staff, past and present, who have made Verveine what it is today, I can't thank you enough for consistently going above and beyond.

To all the guests who have supported Verveine and shown such enthusiasm and gusto – thank you.

Thanks to the suppliers who provide us with the freshest and finest ingredients, not forgetting the workers all over the world that we often take for granted, who harvest and process spices in difficult and often dangerous parts of the world.

Thank you to David Nash of The Electric Eye for the incredible photography.

To Martin Edwards and Steve Levers for making this book way more than I hoped it would be.

To Hilary Linda and Nick Vowles who created our stunning resin art table tops.

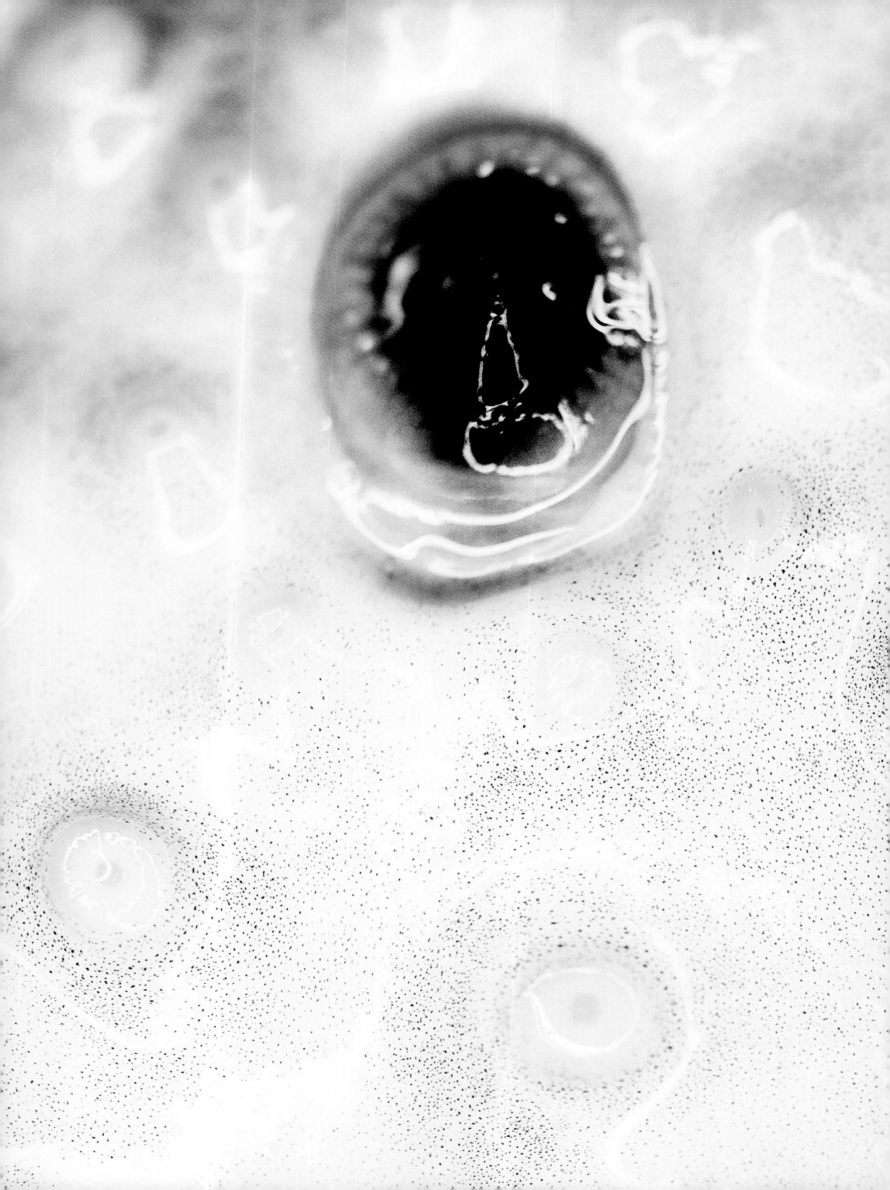

"You're only given a little spark of madness
and if you lose that, you're nothing"
ROBIN WILLIAMS

# INDEX

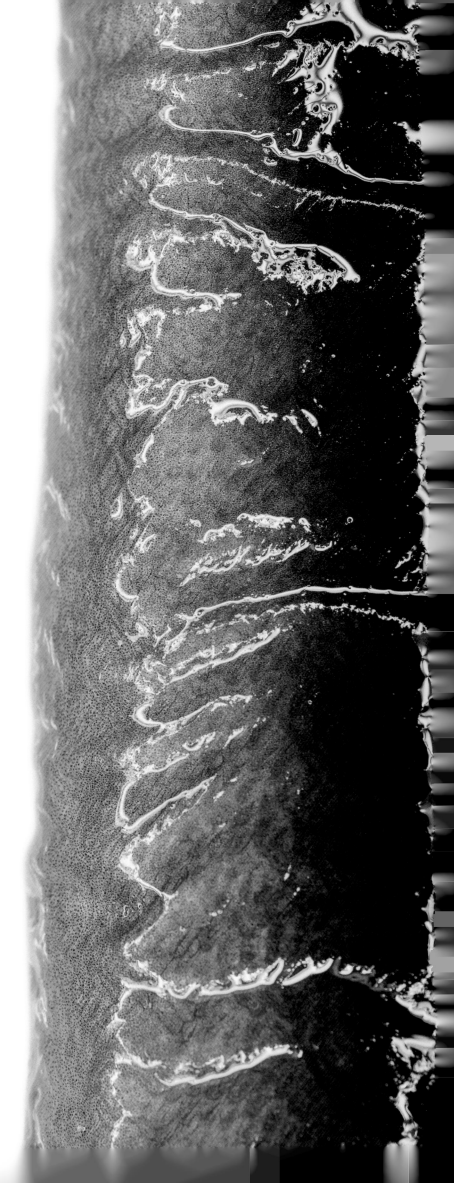

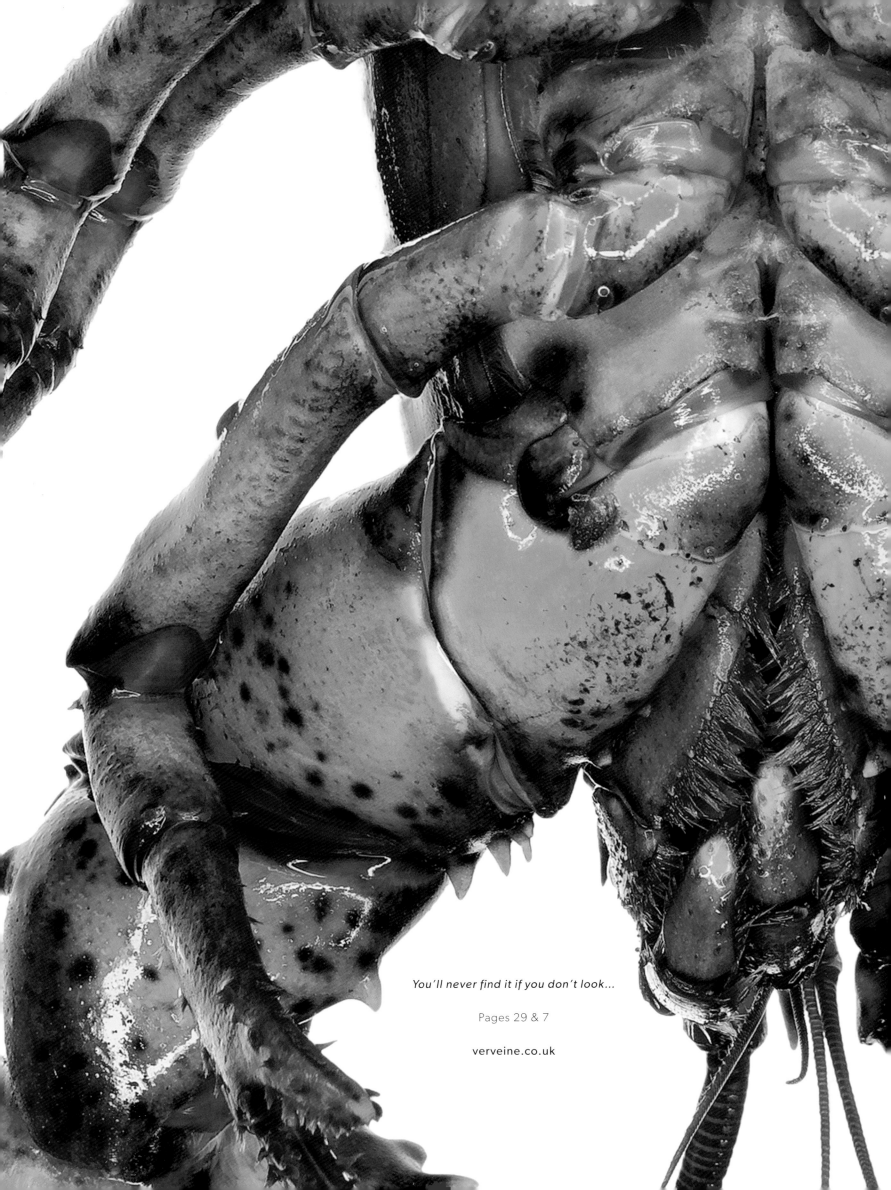

*You'll never find it if you don't look...*

Pages 29 & 7

verveine.co.uk